Lilly Higgins'   *Dream Deli*

Lilly Higgins'

DREAM DELI

gill & macmillan

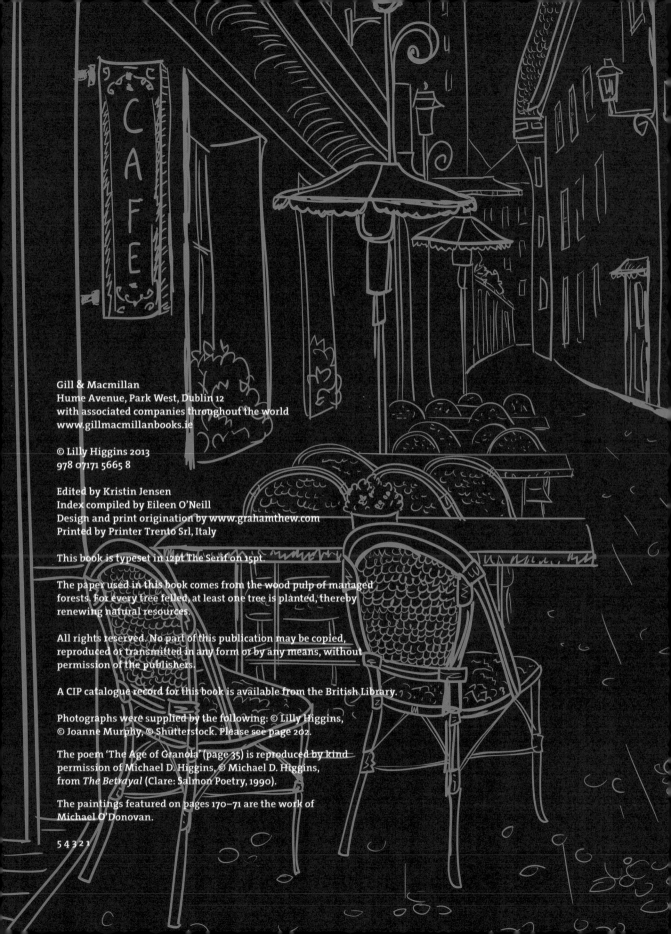

Gill & Macmillan
Hume Avenue, Park West, Dublin 12
with associated companies throughout the world
www.gillmacmillanbooks.ie

© Lilly Higgins 2013
978 07171 5665 8

Edited by Kristin Jensen
Index compiled by Eileen O'Neill
Design and print origination by www.grahamthew.com
Printed by Printer Trento Srl, Italy

This book is typeset in 12pt The Serif on 15pt.

The paper used in this book comes from the wood pulp of managed
forests. For every tree felled, at least one tree is planted, thereby
renewing natural resources.

A CIP catalogue record for this book is available from the British Library.

Photographs were supplied by the following: © Lilly Higgins,
© Joanne Murphy, © Shutterstock. Please see page 202.

The poem 'The Age of Granola' (page 35) is reproduced by kind
permission of Michael D. Higgins, © Michael D. Higgins,
from *The Betrayal* (Clare: Salmon Poetry, 1990).

The paintings featured on pages 170–71 are the work of
Michael O'Donovan.

5 4 3 2 1

CONTENTS

LUNCH and SUPPER

TEA BREAK and DESSERTS

SIDES and EXTRAS

ACKNOWLEDGEMENTS

It was great to have the same team working with me from Gill & Macmillan for this, my second book. Thanks so much to Fergal Tobin, D Rennison Kunz and Teresa Daly and especially to Nicki Howard for your belief and encouragement. Thanks to the talented Graham Thew for bringing my photographs to life with your beautiful design skills and making each page unique. Thanks also to the lovely Joanne Murphy and your team for taking the photos of me.

Once again I was lucky to have Kristin Jensen copyedit my recipes. It's a food blogger's dream to have such a talented fellow blogger to work with.

Thanks to Petria and Maisha Lenehan for being so lovely and letting us take over your gorgeous café, Bibi's Café and Dolls Boutique, for our photos.

Thanks to all at Ballymaloe and to Darina Allen for your never-ending support and enthusiasm and for passing on your passion for Irish food.

Thanks to all my lovely blog readers! This all started with my blog and I hope ye continue with me on this culinary journey.

To all the O'Donovan family, especially Eimear. Thanks so much for your support.

Thanks to my amazing parents, Dave and Monica, and to my inspiring siblings. Ye are all so good to listen to me chatting about recipes on Skype or at the kitchen table and helping me to test everything! I would be lost without your encouragement, inspiration and love. Thanks so much to you all.

To my beautiful little niece Aoibhinn, for being incredibly honest when you taste something and letting me know if you like it or not (no! no! no!). You'll love that carrot soup when you're big!

And thanks to Colm, love of my life. Since the last book we have had two amazing baby boys and it definitely has been hectic, but also so enjoyable with you by my side.

Finally, thanks to my two gorgeous boys, Liam and Cathal. Liam: tea brack, butterbeans and black pudding will make you big and strong, keep it up! Thanks for helping me so much in the kitchen. You're the best boy. Cathal, you're such a little sweetie and thanks for being so smiley and easygoing. You're the best little baby. Ye are truly amazing and I love ye both. xxx

INTRODUCTION

I graduated from Ballymaloe Cookery School in 2007, inspired and confident from my time there. I was sure that within a year, I would open up my dream restaurant and it would be a big hit. It's a starry-eyed dream that so many people have. You love food and want to share it? Me too! I had met the boy of my dreams and the Celtic Tiger was in full swing. Oh, how things have changed! Well, some things. The dream boy is still here and we have two baby boys of our own. Alas, the Tiger has long since left us to stalk around new lands, probably enjoying gorgeous weather and impeccable restaurant service!

So I worked in an office and spent my evenings and weekends writing recipes and photographing food for my blog. I got so much pleasure from food blogging; I'd recommend it to anyone. Soon, though, describing the aroma of cumin-dusted roast pumpkin or the texture of a duck egg sponge wasn't enough – I wanted to actually cook for lots of people, outside of my family. I longed to serve up some tasty grub and see people's reactions there and then.

The dream of opening a restaurant had resurfaced and I had to act on it. So I put an invitation on the blog for readers to come to dinner and called the evening the Loaves and Fishes Supper Club. Coming from a family of ten, I'm used to cooking for large numbers and loved the idea of scaling right up to a mammoth family-style chow down. I bought lots of old chairs and pretty crockery from charity shops and rented three huge tables. I enlisted the help of my sisters and friends and we began to hold monthly suppers in a Dublin home. I packed the car with ingredients from the English Market in Cork and my invaluable food processor. Once a month for a year, my sister Rosie drove with me to Dublin and on the way, we'd talk through the menu and plan the evening ahead. When would we fill the glasses with the elderflower and cucumber champagne? Which plates would we use to serve the chola tikki? Who would get the fun job of rolling the chocolate and chilli truffles and who'd be stuck ironing the napkins? Figuring out each detail and task involved in feeding a crowd from a family home was hard work, but really exciting and fun too. My sisters were fantastic and we really enjoyed working on it together. I was sorry to finish up Loaves and Fishes, but I always knew that the suppers, by their nature, had to pop down as well as pop up!

The supper club was the perfect way of dipping my toe in the restaurant scene in a noncommittal way. I've never stopped compiling recipes and dreaming of a place of my own to serve delicious food in a beautiful atmosphere to other food lovers. That place turned out to be this book – a collection of recipes that would be on the menu of my Dream Delicatessen.

I've been imagining this place for so long and I'm thrilled to have brought it to life in these pages. I've loved working out the perfect recipes to share with you. For me, creating the pop-up restaurant, having my two little boys with Colm, and photographing and writing about food for a living is even more than I dreamed about years ago.

I hope that you take the time to make yourself something delicious to eat and sit with it as you think about your own dreams – they are quite possibly coming true all around you. Now, enough talk. Come on in to my Dream Delicatessen – let's eat!

CONVERSION CHARTS

WEIGHT

30g	1oz	425g	15oz
60g	2oz	450g	1lb
90g	3oz	500g	18oz
110g	4oz	570g	1¼lb
140g	5oz	680g	1½lb
170g	6oz	900g	2lb
200g	7oz	1kg	2¼lb
225g	8oz	1.1kg	2½lb
250g	9oz	1.4kg	3lb
280g	10oz	1.5kg	3lb 5oz
310g	11oz	1.8kg	4lb
340g	12oz	2kg	4¼lb
370g	13oz	2.2kg	5lb
400g	14oz		

VOLUME

5ml	1 teaspoon	240ml	8 fl oz
10ml	1 dessertspoon	270ml	9 fl oz
15ml	1 tablespoon	300ml	10 fl oz
30ml	1 fl oz	325ml	11 fl oz
60ml	2 fl oz	350ml	12 fl oz
90ml	3 fl oz	400ml	14 fl oz
120ml	4 fl oz	425ml	15 fl oz
150ml	5 fl oz	465ml	16 fl oz
175ml	6 fl oz	1 litre	35 fl oz
200ml	7 fl oz		

OVEN

Degrees Celsius	Degrees Fahrenheit	Gas Mark	Description
140	275	1	Very cool
150	300	2	Cool
160	325	3	Warm
180	350	4	Moderate
190	375	5	Fairly hot
200	400	6	Fairly hot
220	425	7	Hot
230	450	8	Very hot
240	475	9	Very hot

BREAKFAST
and BRUNCH

COME ON IN, IT'S TIME TO BREAKFAST LIKE A KING!

Your favourite seat (the one by the window, with the high back and comfy cushion) is waiting. Golden sunrays are creeping across the floorboards, filling the room with warmth. The newspapers are ready for you to read, and there's only good news. Turns out everything is going to be fine. Phew! Now, there's no rush, we promise not to even look you in the eye until after 11 o'clock. All you need to do is order your favourite wake-up coffee, or calm-down tea, and study the menu. The only choice you need to make this morning is which gorgeous dish to order.

The Dream Deli menu has something for everyone. Ease into the morning with a comforting bowl of **CREAMY PORRIDGE**. Indulge in **WAFFLES** or **CRISPY FRENCH TOAST**. If you love pancakes as much as I do, you'll appreciate the **BERRY-FILLED CRÊPES** or plump and pretty **PIKELETS**. The **WINTER FRUIT SALAD** and the revelatory **FRUIT TABBOULEH** are elegant and virtuous, an aspirational start to the day. The indulgent **CHOCOLATE GRANOLA** is almost too tasty to be good for you, yet it's completely sugar free.

For a more substantial brunch, choose the gorgeous and nutritious **OMEGA-3 KEDGEREE** to fill you up with its heartiness. Eggs, glorious eggs, baked to yellow-yolked perfection and paired with a crisp **RÖSTI**, will ensure a wonderful start to your day. And don't forget a drink to wash it all down. There's a **SMOOTHIE** for every occasion, packed full of probiotic yoghurt and fruit. There's no better way to start the day! Treat yourself well, because mornings are tough. Get this meal right, and the rest of the day will fall into place before your smiling eyes.

PORRIDGE with HONEY and TOASTED OATS

200G PORRIDGE OATS + 4 TBSP
EXTRA, FOR TOASTING
- -

400ML MILK
- - - - - - - - - - - - - - -

PINCH OF SALT
- - - - - - - - - - - - - - - -

SOFTLY WHIPPED CREAM, TO SERVE
- -

HONEY, TO SERVE
- - - - - - - - - - - - - - - - - - -

SERVES 4

1 Place a dry frying pan over a medium heat and toast the 4 tablespoons of oats until they're lightly coloured and fragrant. Set aside.

2 Place the 200g of oats, the milk and 800ml water into a saucepan. Bring to the boil, then lower the heat and stir frequently for 5 minutes. Add the salt and continue to stir for a further 5 minutes, or until the mixture becomes thick and creamy.

3 Ladle the porridge into 4 bowls. Place a dollop of whipped cream in the centre, drizzle with honey and scatter with the toasted oats.

FRENCH TOAST with APPLE COMPÔTE and BLACKBERRIES

1 To make the compôte, place the apple slices in a medium pan along with 2–3 tablespoons water, the lemon juice, cloves and cinnamon stick. Simmer over a low heat for 8–10 minutes, or until the apple is just cooked. Remove the cloves and cinnamon stick and stir in the sugar until it dissolves. Remove the pan from the heat and blitz to a smooth purée using a handheld mixer or liquidiser.

2 To make the French toast, whisk the eggs and milk in a wide, shallow bowl. Soak the bread in the egg mixture 1 slice at a time, shaking off any excess.

3 Melt half the butter in a wide frying pan over a medium heat. Add 3 or 4 slices of the soaked bread in a single layer. Cook until golden brown on both sides. Cook the remaining bread in batches, adding more butter as needed. Keep the cooked slices warm in the oven. Dust generously with icing sugar before serving with the compôte and a handful of blackberries.

FOR THE FRENCH TOAST:

3 EGGS

240ML MILK

8 THICK SLICES OF BRIOCHE OR 4 BRIOCHE ROLLS, HALVED

60G BUTTER

ICING SUGAR, FOR DUSTING

100–150G BLACKBERRIES

FOR THE COMPÔTE:

6 MEDIUM EATING APPLES, PEELED, CORED AND SLICED

JUICE OF 1 LEMON

2 CLOVES

1 SMALL CINNAMON STICK

100G CASTER SUGAR

SERVES 4

OPTIONS:

○ Use plump sultana-studded fruit loaf instead of brioche.

○ Add 1 teaspoon ground cinnamon to the melted butter when frying the bread for a spicy, subtle warmth.

WELSH RAREBIT

2 TSP DIJON MUSTARD

60ML STOUT (I LIKE EIGHT DEGREES KNOCKMEALDOWN PORTER)

60G BUTTER

2 TSP WORCESTERSHIRE SAUCE, TO TASTE

350G MATURE FARMHOUSE CHEESE, GRATED

SALT AND FRESHLY GROUND BLACK PEPPER

2 EGGS + 1 EGG YOLK

4 SLICES OF BREAD

SERVES 4

1 Mix the mustard and a little stout to make a paste in a small pan. Add the remaining stout, the butter and the Worcestershire sauce. Gently heat until the butter melts. Stir in the cheese to melt, but don't let the mixture boil. Stir until smooth, then taste for seasoning. Remove from the heat and keep slightly warm while you toast the bread.

2 Heat the grill and toast the bread on both sides. Beat the eggs and yolk into the cheese sauce. Once smooth, spoon it generously onto the toast and grill until bubbling and golden.

OPTIONS:

- Fried bacon and maple syrup
- Fresh blackberries and apple compôte (see page 5)
- Chantilly cream and fleur de sel caramel sauce
- Strawberries and cream
- Raspberries and lightly whipped cream that has been muddled with fresh mint leaves
- Grilled pineapple slices flambéed in rum and a scoop of vanilla ice cream
- Slices of banana and a drizzle of honey

WEEKEND WAFFLES

1 Sift the flour and baking powder together into a large mixing bowl and then stir through the sugar.

2 Whisk the eggs and milk together in a jug and add the melted butter. Make a hollow in the dry ingredients and pour in the egg mixture. Stir until just combined and there are no large lumps of flour.

3 Brush the plates of a preheated electric waffle iron with melted butter. Carefully ladle on the batter, keeping in mind that it will spread to the edges once the iron is closed. Lower the lid and cook until the waffles are fluffy and golden. Keep warm until ready to serve.

300G PLAIN FLOUR

1½ TSP BAKING POWDER

60G DEMERARA SUGAR

2 EGGS

500ML MILK

100G BUTTER, MELTED, PLUS EXTRA FOR COOKING

MAKES 8–10 WAFFLES

CRÊPES with BERRIES

300G PLAIN FLOUR

1 TSP CASTER SUGAR

2 EGGS, LIGHTLY BEATEN

480ML MILK

15G BUTTER, MELTED

SUNFLOWER OIL

350G MIXED BERRIES

ICING SUGAR, TO DUST

SERVES 6

1 Sift the flour and sugar into a bowl, then make a well in the centre.

2 Whisk the eggs and milk together with 2½ tablespoons water. Slowly pour into the well in the dry ingredients, whisking all the time to ensure a smooth batter. Stir in the melted butter. Cover and place in the fridge to rest for 20–30 minutes.

3 Heat a crêpe pan or non-stick frying pan over a medium heat and coat lightly with sunflower oil. Pour in enough batter to form a thin coat on the base of the pan. Cook for 1 minute, or until the crêpe comes away from the side of the pan. Flip over and cook until golden on the other side.

4 Repeat the process with the remaining batter. Stack the crêpes on a warmed plate with a little greaseproof paper or icing sugar between each one. Cover with tin foil.

5 To serve, gently roll a crêpe into an upturned cone shape, fill with berries and place on a plate. Dust lightly with icing sugar and serve immediately.

PIKELETS with GOLDEN SYRUP and GREEK YOGHURT

150G SELF-RAISING FLOUR

1 TBSP CASTER SUGAR

1 EGG

185ML MILK

MELTED BUTTER, TO FRY

1 VANILLA BEAN, HALVED

250ML GREEK YOGHURT

2 TBSP GOLDEN SYRUP

SERVES 4–5

1 Sift the flour and sugar into a bowl.

2 Whisk the egg and milk together, then add to dry ingredients, whisking until smooth.

3 Heat a non-stick frying pan over a medium heat and brush with a little melted butter. Drop level tablespoonfuls of the batter into the pan and cook for 30 seconds, or until bubbles appear on the surface of the pikelets. Turn over and cook the other side for 1 minute, until golden.

4 Meanwhile, scrape the seeds from the halved vanilla bean into the yoghurt and mix well. Gently ripple the golden syrup through the yoghurt and serve with the warm pikelets.

OPTIONS:
- Any syrups, such as agave or maple, work well here too.
- Folding a few tablespoons of raspberry conserve into the yoghurt is also delicious.

CINNAMON and OAT PANCAKES with HONEY and BANANA

1 Place the flour and half the oats plus the sugar, baking powder, salt and cinnamon in the bowl of a food processor. Blitz until the oats are coarsely ground.

2 Whisk the eggs, milk and oil in a large mixing bowl. Add the flour mixture and the remaining oats. Whisk until just combined.

3 Heat a little sunflower oil in a non-stick frying pan over a medium heat. Drop 2–3 tablespoons of the batter into the pan and cook until bubbles appear on the surface of the pancake. Flip the pancake over and cook for a further 1–2 minutes, until golden. Repeat with the remaining batter.

4 Serve the warm pancakes topped with sliced bananas and drizzled with honey.

300G PLAIN FLOUR

200G PORRIDGE OATS

80G LIGHT BROWN SUGAR

1 TBSP BAKING POWDER

1 TSP SALT

½ TSP GROUND CINNAMON

2 EGGS

480ML MILK

80ML SUNFLOWER OIL, PLUS EXTRA FOR FRYING

½ BANANA PER PERSON, SLICED, TO SERVE

HONEY, TO SERVE

MAKES 12

JUGGED KIPPERS

4 KIPPERS

1 LEMON, QUARTERED INTO WEDGES

BUTTERED BROWN BREAD, TO SERVE

SERVES 4

Remove the heads and tails from the fish. Place them head first into a jug. Pour enough boiling water into the jug to fill it, ensuring the kippers stay upright. Cover with a plate and leave for 6–7 minutes. Pour off the water and pat each fish dry with kitchen paper. Serve immediately with a lemon wedge and buttered brown bread.

et handmade

nola for the

o perfect

h toast

cotta

OMEGA-3 KEDGEREE

150G WILD RICE

150G CAMARGUE RED RICE

150G BROWN BASMATI RICE

5 EGGS

50G BUTTER

8 SPRING ONIONS, SLICED
DIAGONALLY

2–3 TSP CURRY POWDER

SALT AND FRESHLY GROUND
BLACK PEPPER

5 TBSP CHOPPED FLAT-LEAF PARSLEY,
PLUS EXTRA TO GARNISH

3 TBSP FINELY CHOPPED CHIVES

6 FILLETS SMOKED MACKEREL,
FLAKED APART

SERVES 6–8

1 First mix all the rice together, then cook in plenty of water for 30–40 minutes, until al dente. Drain and keep warm.

2 Place the eggs in a saucepan and add enough cold water to cover the eggs by 3cm. Bring to the boil, remove from the heat, cover the pan and leave to stand for 12 minutes. Remove the eggs from the water and run under cold water to cool them quickly. Once cooled, peel the eggs and cut into quarters lengthways.

3 Melt the butter in a large saucepan. Add the spring onions and curry powder. Stir on a low heat until the spices are fragrant and warmed through.

4 Add the rice and stir to coat in the butter. Add plenty of salt and freshly ground black pepper.

5 Fold through the herbs and add the flaked fish. Gently tip into a warm serving dish. Arrange the egg quarters on top and scatter with more parsley.

WINTER FRUIT SALAD

1 Place all the dried fruit, cloves, cinnamon stick, star anise, orange zest and honey into a saucepan. Just cover with boiling water. Bring to the boil, lower the heat and simmer for 20 minutes. Top up with more water if necessary.

2 Allow to cool. Remove the whole spices and stir in the orange blossom water.

3 Serve with granola or porridge and a generous dollop of Greek yoghurt. Kept in a sealed jar in the fridge, this fruit salad will be good for up to a week.

200G DRIED FIGS

150G DRIED PRUNES

100G DRIED APRICOTS

100G DRIED BLUEBERRIES

50G DRIED APPLES

2 CLOVES

1 CINNAMON STICK

1 STAR ANISE

ZEST OF 1 ORANGE

2 TBSP HONEY

FEW DROPS OF ORANGE BLOSSOM WATER

SERVES 6

FRUIT TABBOULEH

Use any fruit juice you like for this attractive salad.

500G BULGUR WHEAT

400ML POMEGRANATE JUICE, HEATED

ZEST OF 1 LIME

ZEST OF 1 ORANGE

250G RASPBERRIES

250G BLUEBERRIES

150G BLACKBERRIES

100G FLAKED ALMONDS, TOASTED

20G MINT LEAVES, FINELY SHREDDED

GREEK YOGHURT

HONEY OR AGAVE SYRUP, TO SERVE

SERVES 6–8

1 Mix the bulgur wheat with the hot pomegranate juice and 250ml boiling water in a bowl. Cover tightly with a lid or cling film and leave to steam for 40 minutes.

2 Fluff with a fork, then add the lime and orange zest. Gently fold in the berries, almond flakes and mint.

3 Spoon into bowls and serve with a dollop of Greek yoghurt and drizzle with honey or agave syrup.

CHOCOLATE GRANOLA

300G PORRIDGE OATS

150G DESICCATED COCONUT

50G COCOA POWDER

100ML HONEY, GENTLY WARMED

PINCH OF SEA SALT

120G ALMOND FLAKES, TOASTED

SERVES 6

1 Preheat the oven to 100°C. Line a large baking tray with greaseproof paper.

2 Mix the oats and coconut in a large bowl. Sieve over the cocoa and stir. Add the honey and sea salt and mix until it forms a dry crumble.

3 Spread it out on the prepared baking tray. Bake for 1 hour, or until dry and crumbly. Stir the granola now and then so that it bakes evenly. Leave to cool before folding in the toasted flaked almonds. Store in an airtight container for up to 2 weeks.

PEANUT BUTTER GRANOLA

This recipe is inspired by the gorgeous granola made by fellow food blogger and Ballymaloe graduate Carolanne Rushe (www.carolanneskitchen.com).

380G PORRIDGE OATS

200G CRUNCHY PEANUT BUTTER

90ML MAPLE SYRUP

2 TBSP COCONUT OIL

2 TBSP COCOA POWDER

1 TSP VANILLA ESSENCE

150G ROASTED PEANUTS

SERVES 6–8

1 Preheat the oven to 120°C.

2 Tip the oats into a mixing bowl.

3 Place the peanut butter, maple syrup, coconut oil, cocoa powder and vanilla in a saucepan and heat gently. Once melted together, pour into the oats and stir to combine.

4 Spread the mixture out on a baking tray and bake for 1 hour 15 minutes. Stir every 15 minutes to ensure it bakes evenly and doesn't burn.

5 Once the granola has cooled, stir through the roasted peanuts. Store in an airtight container for up to 2 weeks.

Peanut Butter Granola

Health Farm Granola

Chocolate Granola

Maple and Pecan Nut Granola

PEANUT BUTTER GRANOLA OPTIONS:

This is delicious for breakfast, but it also makes a decadent dessert when sprinkled over a scoop of rich chocolate or caramel ice cream.

HEALTH FARM GRANOLA

300G ROLLED OATS

120G SUNFLOWER SEEDS

80G PUMPKIN SEEDS

70G WHOLE ALMONDS, ROUGHLY CHOPPED

70G BRAZIL NUTS, ROUGHLY CHOPPED

70G HAZELNUTS, ROUGHLY CHOPPED

125ML UNSWEETENED APPLE JUICE

50ML SUNFLOWER OIL

SERVES 6–8

1 Preheat the oven to 160°C.

2 Place all the ingredients in a large bowl and mix until well combined. Spread out evenly on a baking tray and bake for 1 hour. Stir the granola every 15 minutes to ensure it's baking evenly and not burning.

3 Once cooled, store in an airtight container for up to 2 weeks.

OPTIONS:

° *Once cooled, stir through dried fruits such as sultanas, raisins or figs.*

° *Serve with yoghurt or layer it like a sundae with berries, honey and yoghurt for a healthy dessert.*

MAPLE and PECAN NUT GRANOLA

400G PORRIDGE OATS

150G PECAN NUTS

250ML MAPLE SYRUP

125ML SUNFLOWER OIL

SERVES 8–10

1 Preheat the oven to 160°C.

2 Place the oats and nuts into a large mixing bowl.

3 Gently heat the maple syrup and oil along with 125ml water. Bring to the boil, then pour into the oat mixture. Stir to combine.

4 Spread out evenly on a baking tray and bake for 1 hour. Stir the granola every 15 minutes to ensure it's baking evenly. Lower the heat to 140°C and continue to bake for 1 hour more. Again, check it regularly.

5 Once cooled, store in an airtight container for up to 2 weeks.

QUINOA and CHIA SEED GRANOLA

300G PORRIDGE OATS

120G QUINOA (UNCOOKED)

120G PECAN NUTS, ROUGHLY CHOPPED

80G CHIA SEEDS

50G SESAME SEEDS

50G PUMPKIN SEEDS

50G SUNFLOWER SEEDS

100ML MAPLE SYRUP

100ML SUNFLOWER OIL

SERVES 6–8

1 Preheat the oven to 200°C. Line 2 baking sheets with greaseproof paper.

2 Mix all the dry ingredients together. Pour over the maple syrup and sunflower oil. Stir well to combine.

3 Spread the mixture over the lined baking sheets, flattening it with the back of a spoon to create an even surface. Bake for about 40 minutes, until uniformly golden. Stir every 10 minutes to ensure the seeds and nuts aren't burning. Leave to cool completely on the trays before storing in an airtight container for up to 2 weeks.

The AGE of GRANOLA

It was in the age of Granola
When you had long flowing hair
And people turned when we laughed
For they deeply coveted the reason
That we with so little
Were free

It was in the age of Granola
That our bodies were supple and thin
And our friends kept asking you how you did it,
You had such beautiful skin.
But at night you told them of Miso,
On buses they wondered
When you went all serious about Zen.

It was in the age of Granola
When you wore a massive black hat,
That I burned the rubbish of guilt
And it really didn't take much effort
For love to find its way in.

And that's why we never really saw it,
The wave that was coming our way.

In Moscow they're queuing for McDonald's
In Tokyo Bud is the choice
And freedom brings pills to the South.
And we never saw that it was coming,
The whole world was going to be free.

BIRCHER MUESLI

1 ORANGE

1 GRAPEFRUIT

1 LIME

200G PORRIDGE OATS

50G RAISINS

1 LARGE EATING APPLE, GRATED

50ML YOGHURT

2 TBSP AGAVE SYRUP OR HONEY

SERVES 4

1 Juice the citrus fruit – there should be approximately 300ml juice in total.

2 Place the juice, oats and raisins into a mixing bowl. Stir to combine. Cover with cling film and leave to soak in the fridge for at least half an hour, or ideally overnight.

3 Stir the grated apple, yoghurt and agave syrup through just before serving.

FRUIT PLATTER

This is more of an assembly job than a recipe. Simply choose fruits that will work well together and prepare them so they are ready to eat. Pretty miniature fruit is sometimes available, such as bananas and pineapples. This makes a stunning edible centrepiece for a celebratory breakfast table.

MANGO, DESTONED AND CUT INTO WEDGES

SPRIGS OF GRAPES

WEDGES OF MELON

THICK SLICES OF KIWI

PASSIONFRUIT, HALVED

GRAPEFRUIT SEGMENTS

FRESH PINEAPPLE BATONS

DRAGON FRUIT, CUT INTO WEDGES

KIWANO, HALVED

APPLES, DECORED AND CUT INTO WEDGES

MANDARIN ORANGES, PEELED AND LEFT WHOLE

LARGE BERRIES SUCH AS STRAWBERRIES

CHERRIES

PEARS, DECORED AND CUT INTO WEDGES

PEACHES, DESTONED AND QUARTERED

NECTARINES, DESTONED AND HALVED

HOMEMADE YOGHURT

Use full-fat and organic milk and yoghurt if you can. The dried milk powder is not entirely necessary, but it makes the yoghurt creamier.

500ML MILK

30G DRIED MILK POWDER

50ML NATURAL YOGHURT

MAKES 500G YOGHURT

1 Pour the milk into a heavy-bottomed saucepan and whisk through the powdered milk. Heat until it almost comes to the boil. Watch carefully, as milk can bubble over in seconds. Remove from the heat and pour into a wide mixing bowl, then leave to cool until it reaches body temperature. A thermometer is very handy here, as the temperature will be about 40°C when it's ready. This can take 30–40 minutes.

2 Whisk the natural yoghurt through the warm milk, then cover the bowl with cling film, wrap it in towels and leave in a warm place for 8 hours or overnight. Alternatively, you could keep the mixture warm in a wide-mouthed Thermos flask. By morning, the mixture will have thickened into yoghurt. Keep in the fridge. If you would like thicker yoghurt, you can strain it through a muslin cloth.

3 Once your yoghurt is made, you can place it into little jars and ripple it with fruit purée, sweeten it with honey and scrape vanilla seeds into it or serve it with toasted almonds and a drizzle of honey for a protein-rich breakfast or tasty dessert.

BAKED EGGS with WILTED SPINACH and PARMA HAM

1 Preheat the oven to 180°C. Butter 6 ovenproof ramekins.

2 Place the spinach in a pan with the butter over a medium heat and stir until wilted. Remove any excess liquid from the spinach and roughly chop into bite-sized pieces.

3 Divide the spinach evenly between the 6 ramekins. Next, top with the Parma ham and the tomatoes. Crack an egg into each ramekin. Top with 2 tablespoons of cream and a generous amount of black pepper. Lastly, add some Parmesan shavings.

4 Place the ramekins into a roasting dish. Place the dish on the oven shelf and pour boiling water into the roasting dish to create a bain marie. Pour in enough water so that it comes halfway up the sides of the ramekins. Cook for 10–15 minutes, depending on the depth of the dishes. Ensure the egg white is set and the yolk is still a little soft. Garnish with parsley and serve with sourdough bread.

250G SPINACH

15G BUTTER

90G PARMA HAM, TORN INTO BITE-SIZED PIECES

150G CHERRY TOMATOES, QUARTERED

6 EGGS

180ML CREAM

FRESHLY GROUND BLACK PEPPER

PARMESAN SHAVINGS

SOURDOUGH BREAD, TO SERVE

FRESH FLAT-LEAF PARSLEY LEAVES, TO GARNISH

SERVES 6

OPTIONS:

○ Slices of fried chorizo and halved cherry tomatoes

○ Torn pieces of hot smoked salmon and crème fraîche

SPICED BEETROOT and POTATO RÖSTI

200ML GREEK YOGHURT

2 TBSP POMEGRANATE MOLASSES

1.3KG POTATOES (ROOSTER OR SIMILAR), PEELED AND ROUGHLY GRATED

800G PRE-COOKED BEETROOT, ROUGHLY GRATED

2 TBSP SALT

4 CLOVES GARLIC, CRUSHED

6 TBSP OLIVE OIL

4 TBSP CHOPPED CHIVES

4 TSP GROUND CUMIN

FRESHLY GROUND BLACK PEPPER

6 FRIED EGGS, TO SERVE

SERVES 6 (MAKES 12 RÖSTI)

1 Preheat the oven to 200°C. Line 2 baking trays with greaseproof paper.

2 Place the yoghurt in a bowl and gently stir through the molasses. Cover and refrigerate.

3 Place a tea towel in a colander and sit it into the sink. Tip the potaoes and grated beetroot into the tea towel and sprinkle the salt over. Gather all four corners of the towel and squeeze the bundle to get as much liquid out as possible. Leave to sit for 5 minutes before squeezing again. Try to get the mixture as dry as possible. Shake the vegetables out of the towel and place them in a large bowl with the garlic, olive oil, chives, cumin and black pepper. Stir to combine.

4 Place 6 mounds of the potato mix on each tray. Use a circular biscuit cutter to achieve a uniform shape if it helps. Usually the rougher the edges, the crispier it becomes. Don't pack the mixture down tightly, as it won't cook evenly. Leave the mixture a little loose and it will settle as it cooks.

5 Cook for 40–45 minutes, rotating the trays halfway through, until the rösti are crisp and golden. Serve immediately with the yoghurt and a fried egg on top.

OPTIONS:

○ Make plain rösti by using the ingredients above but omitting the beetroot and spices.

○ Potato and apple rösti with black pudding: Add 1 apple, grated and squeezed dry, to the plain rösti mixture. Serve with black pudding and hot mustard.

○ Potato rösti with chorizo and fried duck egg: Fry chorizo slices until crispy and serve with a fried duck egg.

○ Potato rösti with smoked salmon, crème fraîche and cucumber pickle.

SMOOTHIES

There's a smoothie for every occasion here. If you need to be gently roused from slumber, then the subtle, floral-scented Raspberry Smoothie is the nicest way to start the day. Or if you're in a tizzy with a long day ahead, then jump right in with the Mocha Smoothie. After a long run or even a strenuous shopping trip, the protein- and potassium-rich Recovery Smoothie is the one for you!

Feel free to add or take away any ingredients here. Generally speaking I use bananas, oats or soaked chia seeds to thicken my smoothies. Using frozen fruit and berries also gives it that distinctive thicker texture. Agave syrup and honey are perfect sweeteners.

All these smoothies are made the same way: just throw everything into a blender and blitz till smooth. Any leftovers can be stored in the fridge for the following day – just shake well before serving.

RASPBERRY, ROSEWATER and CHIA SEED

100G FROZEN RASPBERRIES

200ML MILK

50ML NATURAL YOGHURT

1 TBSP CHIA SEEDS, GROUND AND SOAKED FOR 10 MINUTES IN 1 TBSP WATER

1 TSP HONEY

1/4 TSP ROSEWATER

SERVES 1–2

DATE and VANILLA

60G (8–9) DATES, PITTED

200ML MILK

100ML NATURAL YOGHURT

2 TBSP PORRIDGE OATS

1/2 TSP VANILLA PASTE

SERVES 1–2

BLUEBERRY and LIME

1 BANANA

ZEST OF ½ LIME

150ML BLUEBERRY YOGHURT

2 TSP LIME JUICE

SERVES 1

MORNING MOCHA

200ML MILK

150ML COLD COFFEE

100ML YOGHURT

4 TBSP OATS

1 TBSP AGAVE SYRUP

1 TSP COCOA POWDER

SERVES 1–2

RECOVERY SMOOTHIE

1 BANANA

100ML MILK

2 TBSP CRUNCHY PEANUT BUTTER

1 TSP HONEY

SERVES 1

LILLY'S DREAM DELI

table 4

1·6

2 X STAR
ANISE SOUP

3 X BEAN
BURGERS

PEA
SO...

LUNCH and SUPPER

IT'S THE MIDDLE OF THE DAY. YOU NEED A BREAK AFTER HOURS OF WORKING FOR THE MAN.

Remove yourself for an hour and grab some super-powerful me time! Big, punchy salads like the **LENTIL AND AVOCADO SALAD** or the **QUINOA SALAD WITH PISTACHIOS AND POMEGRANATE** will restore your equilibrium and slowly release energy for the next few hours, so you can go back to work recharged and calm. Please taste the **CARROT AND STAR ANISE SOUP**. It's amazing, though I say so myself. The herb-heavy, flavourful **TABBOULEH** and the **MANGO AND SHREDDED CHICKEN SALAD** are a thousand times more delicious than any canteen food or petrol station sandwich, so fill your lunchbox and bask happily in your colleagues' envy.

The **FETA STUFFED FALAFEL BURGER** and the **SPICY BLACK BEAN BURGER** taste incredible. Stuffed into a pitta bread and served with a side of salad leaves, they're a quick crowd-pleaser, loved by all that try them.

Meeting a group of pals? Lucky you! The thick-cut **SOURDOUGH TOASTS**, laden with tasty toppings like crab and ginger or avocado, lime and red onion, are a cool alternative to conventional sandwiches. Share a board of these toasts with a few shots of soup and your lunchtime gang will liven up, quick sharp.

All these dishes make super suppers too. The **OLD SCHOOL SUNDAY SALAD** is a nostalgic, fuss-free dish that's perfect for lazy Sunday evenings. The **PLOUGHMAN'S PLATTER** can be prepared in minutes. Working as a harmonious flavour collective, the balance of sweet pickles, salty ham and nutty cheddar never fails to satisfy. Do your worst, Afternoon, this happy customer is ready to face whatever you've got in store!

TABBOULEH

150G BULGUR WHEAT

80G PARSLEY

60G MINT

1 MEDIUM RED ONION,
FINELY DICED

JUICE OF 1 LEMON

80ML OLIVE OIL

2 TOMATOES, FINELY DICED

SALT AND FRESHLY GROUND
BLACK PEPPER

SERVES 4–6

1 Place the bulgur wheat in a bowl and cover with 200ml boiling water. Cover the bowl with a plate and leave to soak for 30–40 minutes, or until al dente. Fluff with a fork.

2 Pick the leaves from the parsley and mint and discard the stems. Finely chop the herbs and place in a large bowl. Add the finely diced red onion, lemon juice and oil.

3 Once the wheat is ready, add it to the herbs and onion along with the tomatoes. Mix and season well with salt and pepper.

CARROT and SESAME SALAD

1 Place the oils, lemon juice, honey, spices and seasoning into a jar or lidded container. Shake until mixed.

2 Pour the dressing over the grated carrots. Sprinkle generously with the sesame seeds and parsley just before serving.

4 TBSP OLIVE OR RAPESEED OIL

4 TBSP LEMON JUICE

1 TSP SESAME OIL

½ TSP HONEY

PINCH OF GROUND CUMIN

PINCH OF GROUND CORIANDER

SALT AND FRESHLY GROUND BLACK PEPPER

500G CARROTS, PEELED AND GRATED

50G SESAME SEEDS, TOASTED

2 TBSP VERY FINELY CHOPPED FLAT-LEAF PARSLEY

SERVES 6

FENNEL and CUCUMBER SALAD

1 Trim the fronds from the fennel bulbs and reserve. Using a sharp knife or mandoline, thinly slice the fennel bulbs and red onion.

2 Use a peeler to shave the cucumber into thin strips lengthways. Lay the strips on kitchen paper and pat away any excess moisture.

3 Combine the fennel, onion and cucumber in a large bowl. Season generously with salt and pepper and dress with the lemon juice and oil. Finely chop the reserved fennel fronds and scatter over the salad. Let the flavours develop for at least 30 minutes before serving.

2 FENNEL BULBS

1 RED ONION

1 CUCUMBER

SALT AND FRESHLY GROUND BLACK PEPPER

3 TBSP LEMON JUICE

2 TBSP OLIVE OIL

SERVES 4–6

OLD SCHOOL SUNDAY SALAD

This nostalgic salad is perfect for teatime on a summer Sunday when cooking seems like too much effort!

1 Place the eggs in a saucepan and add enough cold water to cover the eggs by 3cm. Bring to the boil, remove from the heat, cover the pan and leave to stand for 12 minutes. Remove the eggs from the water and run under cold water to cool them quickly. Once cooled, peel the eggs and cut in half lengthways.

2 Divide the lettuce between 6 plates. Place 3 spring onions, 2 egg halves, 1 slice of cheese, 1 slice of ham, half a tomato and 2 slices of bread on each plate. Spoon a dollop of salad cream on the side.

1 BUTTERHEAD LETTUCE, LEAVES TORN INTO BITE-SIZED PIECES

18 MINIATURE SPRING ONIONS

6 EGGS

6 SLICES CHEDDAR CHEESE

6 SLICES HAM

3 TOMATOES, HALVED

12 SLICES WHITE BREAD, BUTTERED AND CUT INTO TRIANGLES

6 TBSP SALAD CREAM

SERVES 6

QUINOA SALAD with PISTACHIOS and POMEGRANATE

You can use any sprouted seeds or peppery rocket or watercress instead of the brocco shoots.

650G BUTTERNUT SQUASH, PEELED AND CUT INTO 1CM CUBES

----

3 TBSP OLIVE OIL

200G QUINOA

----

1 TSP GROUND CUMIN

----

1 TSP GROUND CORIANDER

----

1 TSP SUMAC

450ML STOCK OR WATER

120G PISTACHIOS, SHELLED, TOASTED AND CHOPPED

50G BROCCO SHOOTS (A MIXTURE OF ALFALFA, BROCCOLI, CLOVER AND RADISH SPROUTS)

20G FLAT-LEAF PARSLEY, FINELY CHOPPED

SALT AND FRESHLY GROUND BLACK PEPPER

1–2 POMEGRANATES, SEEDS ONLY

SERVES 6

1 Preheat the oven to 200°C.

2 Toss the cubed butternut squash in the olive oil and place in a roasting tin. Roast for 20–25 minutes, until golden around the edges. Stir halfway through the cooking time to ensure an even colour.

3 Place the quinoa in a medium pan and dry fry with no oil over a high heat for a minute or so. Add the spices and stir to coat evenly, then pour over the stock. Bring to the boil, cover and reduce the heat to low. Simmer for 5 minutes, then remove from the heat and leave to stand with the lid on for a further 30 minutes.

4 Fluff the quinoa with a fork and gently mix through the pistachios, brocco shoots, parsley and butternut squash cubes. Season with salt and pepper to taste. Scatter the pomegranate seeds over the top before serving.

MANGO and SHREDDED CHICKEN SALAD with GARAM MASALA YOGHURT

4 COOKED CHICKEN BREASTS OR 280G COOKED CHICKEN, SHREDDED

2 RIPE MANGOS, PEELED AND CUBED

1 RED PEPPER, SLICED INTO STRIPS

1 RED ONION, THINLY SLICED

200ML GREEK YOGHURT

JUICE OF ½ LIME

1 TBSP MANGO CHUTNEY

2 TSP GARAM MASALA

1 TSP NIGELLA SEEDS

30G CORIANDER LEAVES, CHOPPED

SALT

200G MIXED SALAD LEAVES

100G COCONUT CHIPS, TOASTED

SERVES 6

1 Carefully mix the shredded chicken, mangos, pepper and red onion together in a large bowl.

2 Combine the yoghurt, lime juice, mango chutney, garam masala and nigella seeds. Finely chop 2 tablespoons of the coriander and mix it into the yoghurt. Add salt to taste. Add the remaining coriander to the chicken.

3 To assemble, place a large handful of salad leaves on each plate. Top with the chicken and sprinkle the coconut chips over. Drizzle the yoghurt over the salad or serve on the side.

PLOUGHMAN'S PLATTER

SLICED HOME-COOKED HAM
(SEE OPPOSITE)

IRISH FARMHOUSE CHEESE, SUCH
AS HEGARTY'S CHEDDAR

PICKLES – GHERKINS, CORNICHONS AND
PICKLED ONIONS

SOURDOUGH BREAD, THICKLY SLICED

CHERRY TOMATOES

SEEDLESS GRAPES

SALAD LEAVES

TOMATO CHUTNEY

PICCALILLI

Arrange the ham, cheese, pickles, bread, tomatoes, grapes and salad leaves on a wooden carving board. Serve with the chutney and piccalilli.

HAM COOKED in CIDER

750G SMOKED HAM

500ML CIDER
----

6 ALLSPICE BERRIES
----

4 CLOVES

SERVES 6–8

Place everything in a heavy-based pot and bring to the boil. Lower the heat and cook the ham for 45 minutes per kg plus 30 minutes on top of that (a 750g ham will take 1 hour to cook). Once cooked, leave the ham to cool in the cider before removing and carving.

LENTIL and AVOCADO SALAD

1 Put all the dressing ingredients in a jar or lidded container. Shake well to mix.

2 Drain the lentils and rinse well, then place in a large bowl. Add the chopped red onion, red pepper and coriander.

3 Add a little dressing to the salad and toss until the lentils are glistening. Finally, add the tomatoes and avocado and crumble over the feta. Serve immediately.

FOR THE SALAD:

2 X 400G TINS OF PUY LENTILS

1 RED ONION, FINELY CHOPPED

1 RED PEPPER, ROASTED AND FINELY CHOPPED

2 TBSP FINELY CHOPPED CORIANDER

2 TOMATOES, DESEEDED AND CHOPPED

1 AVOCADO, HALVED, PEELED AND CUT INTO CUBES

200G FETA CHEESE

FOR THE DRESSING:

1 CLOVE GARLIC, CRUSHED

90ML OLIVE OIL

30ML BALSAMIC VINEGAR

1/2 TSP HONEY

1/2 TSP DIJON MUSTARD

SERVES 4–6

FOR THE DILL YOGHURT:

500ML GREEK YOGHURT

1 CLOVE GARLIC, CRUSHED

2 TBSP LEMON JUICE

1 TBSP DRIED DILL

SALT

FOR THE BURGERS:

2 CLOVES GARLIC

2 X 400G TINS OF CHICKPEAS, DRAINED AND RINSED

1 RED ONION, ROUGHLY CHOPPED

1 SMALL BUNCH OF FRESH CORIANDER, LEAVES AND STALKS ROUGHLY CHOPPED

70G PLAIN FLOUR

2 TSP GROUND CORIANDER

1 TSP GROUND CUMIN

½ TSP CHILLI POWDER

SALT AND FRESHLY GROUND BLACK PEPPER

200G FETA CHEESE

3 TBSP SUNFLOWER OIL

8 WHOLEMEAL PITTA BREADS, TOASTED

THICKLY CUT TOMATO SLICES, TO SERVE

CARROT STRIPS, TO SERVE

CUCUMBER STRIPS, TO SERVE

MAKES 8

FETA STUFFED FALAFEL BURGERS

1 First make the dill yoghurt. Combine the yoghurt, garlic, lemon juice and dill. Add salt to taste, cover and set aside.

2 To make the burgers, place the garlic in a food processor and blend until finely chopped. Add the drained chickpeas, onion, fresh coriander, flour, spices and a sprinkling of salt and pepper. Blend on high until well mixed – you may need to stop and scrape down the sides of the bowl a few times to avoid half the mixture becoming too smooth and half too rough.

3 Cut the block of feta cheese into 8 equal squares. Divide the falafel mixture into 8 flat discs. Place a square of cheese in the centre and bring up the corners of the falafel disc to envelop it, covering the cheese completely and sealing it into the patty. Repeat with the remaining cheese and falafel discs.

4 Heat the oil in a non-stick frying pan over a medium-high heat. Fry the burgers for about 4 minutes on each side, or until golden. Keep warm in the oven or serve straight away with toasted pitta breads, the dill yoghurt, tomato slices and strips of carrot and cucumber.

SPICY BLACK BEAN BURGERS

1 Place the garlic in a food processor and blitz until it's finely chopped. Add the beans, sweetcorn, coriander, paprika, salt and cayenne pepper. Pulse until the mixture has been combined and some of the corn and beans are puréed. You don't want the entire mixture to become a wet mush, so only blitz it a little. Transfer to a mixing bowl and stir in the egg and cracker crumbs. The mixture should combine nicely into a workable 'dough'. (This whole process can also be done in a bowl with a potato masher or fork.)

2 Using wet hands, shape into 6 equal-sized patties. Place on a plate and cover with cling film. Leave to rest in the fridge for 15–20 minutes.

3 Heat a little olive oil in a heavy-based frying pan over a medium heat. Fry the burgers for about 4 minutes on each side, until golden.

4 Serve in warmed bread rolls with sweet potato wedges, salad, sour cream and guacamole.

2 CLOVES GARLIC

460G COOKED BLACK BEANS (2 X 400G TINS, DRAINED)

200G SWEETCORN

20G FRESH CORIANDER, STALKS AND LEAVES FINELY CHOPPED

1 TSP SMOKED PAPRIKA

1 TSP SMOKED OR REGULAR SEA SALT

¼ TSP CAYENNE PEPPER

1 EGG, WHISKED

180G CREAM CRACKERS, CRUSHED

OLIVE OIL

WARM BREAD ROLLS, TO SERVE

SWEET POTATO WEDGES, TO SERVE

SALAD, TO SERVE

SOUR CREAM, TO SERVE

GUACAMOLE, TO SERVE

MAKES 6

VEGETABLE and LAMB MINI MEATLOAVES

1 TBSP OLIVE OIL

1 ONION, FINELY CHOPPED

250G CARROTS, PEELED AND CUBED

1 COURGETTE, CUBED

640G MINCED LAMB

100G SEMI-SUNDRIED TOMATOES, FINELY CHOPPED

30G CORIANDER, FINELY CHOPPED

3 TSP SMOKED PAPRIKA

2 TSP FRESHLY GROUND BLACK PEPPER

2 TSP SUMAC

1½ TSP GROUND CINNAMON

1 TSP SALT

1 TSP GROUND CUMIN

2 EGGS, LIGHTLY BEATEN

CARROT AND SESAME SALAD (PAGE 60), TO SERVE

TZATZIKI (PAGE 180), TO SERVE

MAKES 8 LARGE MUFFIN-SIZED PORTIONS

1 Preheat the oven to 180°C. Line a large muffin tin with greaseproof paper or grease with a little olive oil.

2 Pour the olive oil into a large frying pan set over a medium heat. Add the onion and carrots and sauté for a few minutes before adding the courgette. Sauté for a further 3–5 minutes, until the onion has softened. Leave to cool.

3 Mix together the lamb, sundried tomatoes, chopped coriander and spices in a large bowl. Add the cooled sautéed vegetables and the eggs. Mix until well combined.

4 Pack the mixture into the muffin cups and bake for 30 minutes, until golden on top. Serve with Carrot and Sesame Salad (page 60) and Tzatziki (page 180).

FENNEL, PORK and APPLE SAUSAGE ROLLS

1 First make the pastry. Place the flour and butter into a food processor and combine until it resembles coarse breadcrumbs. Slowly add the water until it forms a dough. Stop once it comes together. This can also be done by hand, using a round-bladed knife or using your fingers to mix. Flatten the dough into a disc, wrap in cling film and chill in the fridge for 30 minutes.

2 Preheat the oven to 220°C. Line a baking tray with parchment paper.

3 Mix together the sausage meat, grated apples, fennel seeds, mustard and some salt and pepper until well combined.

4 Roll the pastry out on a floured surface until it's about ½ cm thick and in the shape of a large, long rectangle. Mould the meat into a sausage shape as long as the pastry and place on one long side of the strip. Brush the edge with the egg wash and fold over to seal and enclose the meat. Divide into 8 individual rolls, brush the tops with egg wash, sprinkle with fennel seeds and place on the lined baking tray.

5 Bake for 25–30 minutes, until golden and cooked through. Cool on a rack.

FOR THE PASTRY:

300G PLAIN FLOUR

160G BUTTER, COLD AND CUBED

70ML ICE-COLD WATER

FOR THE FILLING:

500G GOOD-QUALITY SAUSAGE MEAT

2 APPLES, COARSELY GRATED

2 TSP FENNEL SEEDS, TOASTED AND LIGHTLY CRUSHED, PLUS EXTRA TO GARNISH

1 TSP DIJON MUSTARD

SALT AND FRESHLY GROUND BLACK PEPPER

1 EGG, BEATEN WITH A LITTLE WATER

MAKES 8

TOASTS and TOPPINGS

Simply toast thick slices of good-quality bread on both sides and spread with butter. Spoon these delicious toppings generously onto the toasts and serve immediately.

CRAB and GINGER

2 TBSP GOOD-QUALITY MAYONNAISE

2 TBSP GREEK YOGHURT

1 TBSP LEMON JUICE

1 TSP FRESHLY GRATED GINGER

400G FRESHLY COOKED CRABMEAT

2 FIRM TOMATOES, QUARTERED, DESEEDED AND FINELY DICED

1 TBSP FINELY SNIPPED CHIVES (USE A SCISSORS)

SALT AND FRESHLY GROUND BLACK PEPPER

6 THICK SLICES OF SOURDOUGH BREAD, TOASTED AND BUTTERED

MAKES 6

Mix together the mayonnaise, yoghurt, lemon juice and ginger. Add the crabmeat, tomatoes and chives and mix gently until just combined. Taste for seasoning before spooning onto the toasts.

POACHED SALMON and DILL

400G SKINLESS SALMON FILLET

4 TBSP GOOD-QUALITY MAYONNAISE

2 TBSP LEMON JUICE

1 TBSP GREEK YOGHURT

2 TSP FINELY CHOPPED FRESH DILL

½ TSP FRESHLY GROUND BLACK PEPPER

6 THICK SLICES OF SOURDOUGH BREAD, TOASTED AND BUTTERED

MAKES 6

1 Half fill a small pan with salted water and bring to the boil. Place the salmon into the pan, bring back to the boil and then lower the heat to a bare simmer. Cook for 5–10 minutes depending on the thickness of the fillet. Remove from the heat and leave to rest in the water for a further 5–10 minutes, then remove from the water and flake apart.

2 Mix together the mayonnaise, lemon juice, yoghurt, chopped dill and black pepper. Gently fold in the poached salmon. Taste for seasoning before spooning onto the toasts.

Radish and Smoked Sea Salt

Poached Salmon and Dill

Cheese and Onion

Avocado and Lime

Crab and Ginger

MACKEREL with HORSERADISH BUTTER

6 FRESH MACKEREL FILLETS
----

2 TBSP OLIVE OIL

75G BUTTER

SALT AND FRESHLY GROUND BLACK PEPPER
----

1 TBSP FRESHLY GRATED HORSERADISH
----

6 THICK SLICES OF SOURDOUGH BREAD, TOASTED

LEMON WEDGES, TO SERVE

MAKES 6

1 Dry the mackerel fillets with kitchen paper and remove any bones. Put 1 tablespoon of the oil and 15g of the butter in a large non-stick frying pan over a high heat. Place the mackerel in the pan, skin side down, and season with salt and pepper. Cook for 5–8 minutes, until no pinkness remains in the flesh and the skin is crispy. Repeat with the remaining oil and fillets.

2 Meanwhile, beat the remaining 60g butter and horseradish together until combined.

3 Spread a little horseradish butter onto each slice of toast. Top with a hot mackerel fillet and a squeeze of fresh lemon juice.

AVOCADO and LIME

3 AVOCADOS

JUICE OF 1 LIME
----

6 THICK SLICES OF SOURDOUGH BREAD, TOASTED AND BUTTERED
----

1 RED ONION, VERY FINELY DICED

SALT

MAKES 6

1 Halve the avocados and remove the stone. Cut into slices and squeeze a little lime juice over.

2 Layer the avocado slices onto the buttered toast. Scatter the onion over and sprinkle with a little salt. Serve immediately.

CHEESE and ONION

4 TBSP TOMATO CHUTNEY

6 THICK SLICES OF SOURDOUGH BREAD, TOASTED ON ONE SIDE

1 RED ONION, HALVED AND THINLY SLICED

300G MATURE CHEDDAR CHEESE, GRATED

MAKES 6

Spread the chutney on the untoasted side of bread. Layer the red onion slices on top, sprinkle generously with cheese and place under a hot grill until the cheese has melted. Serve with an additional dollop of chutney.

GOAT CHEESE with RADISH and SMOKED SEA SALT

250G FRESH GOAT CHEESE

6 THICK SLICES OF SOURDOUGH BREAD, TOASTED AND BUTTERED

10–12 RADISHES, THINLY SLICED

2 TBSP OLIVE OIL

SMOKED SEA SALT FLAKES

MAKES 6

Generously spread the goat cheese onto the buttered toast. Top with a few thin radish slices, a drizzle of olive oil and a generous pinch of smoked sea salt.

OPTIONS:
o Add quartered fresh figs and a drizzle of pomegranate molasses on top of the goat cheese.

SALAD SOUP

50G BUTTER

6 SPRING ONIONS, ROUGHLY SLICED

600ML STOCK, HEATED

200G MIXED LETTUCE LEAVES

200G BABY LEAF SPINACH

25G FLAT-LEAF PARSLEY, FINELY CHOPPED

10G MINT LEAVES, FINELY CHOPPED

100ML CREAM

SALT AND FRESHLY GROUND BLACK PEPPER

SERVES 4

Melt the butter in a heavy-based saucepan over a medium heat. Sauté the spring onions for 2–3 minutes, until lightly coloured. Add the hot stock and increase the heat. Add the mixed lettuce, baby spinach and herbs and stir to wilt. After 2 minutes, blend the soup until smooth. Add the cream and salt and pepper to taste. Serve immediately before the lovely green colour fades.

HAM and MARROWFAT PEA SOUP

250G NO-SOAK MARROWFAT PEAS

50G BUTTER

2 LARGE ONIONS, CHOPPED

850ML STOCK OR WATER

250G FROZEN PEAS

250G SMOKED SHREDDED HAM

SALT AND FRESHLY GROUND BLACK PEPPER

SERVES 6

1 Rinse the marrowfat peas in a sieve over the sink to wash off any excess bicarbonate of soda. Place in a medium pan with 1 litre boiling water. Bring to the boil, then lower the heat and cover with a lid. Simmer for 15–20 minutes.

2 In a separate large saucepan, melt the butter over a medium heat and add the onions. Sauté for 5–7 minutes, until softened. Pour in the stock or water and bring to the boil. Add the frozen peas and simmer for 1 minute before adding 200g of the ham. Add the cooked marrowfat peas and their cooking liquor, then blitz until smooth. Taste for seasoning – it shouldn't need much salt due to the ham.

3 When serving the soup, divide the remaining ham between the bowls and ladle the hot soup over.

BEETROOT SOUP with FETA

2 TBSP OLIVE OIL

----

2 ONIONS, FINELY CHOPPED

----

3 CLOVES GARLIC, CRUSHED

½ TSP FENNEL SEEDS, CRUSHED

----

2 X 500G PACKETS OF PRE-COOKED BEETROOT, ROUGHLY CHOPPED

500ML STOCK OR WATER

----

1 TBSP CIDER VINEGAR

----

1 TSP CASTER SUGAR

SALT AND FRESHLY GROUND BLACK PEPPER

150G FETA CHEESE

SERVES 6

1 Heat the olive oil in a large pot over a medium heat. Sauté the chopped onion for 5–7 minutes. Once the onion is soft, add the garlic and fennel seeds. Stir to combine and ensure the garlic doesn't burn.

2 Add the beetroot to the pot, then pour over the stock and vinegar. Bring to the boil and blitz until smooth before adding the sugar, salt and pepper.

3 Ladle into bowls and crumble the cold feta over before serving.

CARROT and STAR ANISE SOUP

50G BUTTER

----

2 ONIONS, CHOPPED

----

6 SPRIGS OF THYME

----

4 WHOLE STAR ANISE

----

2 CLOVES GARLIC, CRUSHED

850G CARROTS, PEELED AND CHOPPED

800ML HOT STOCK

100ML CREAM

SALT AND FRESHLY GROUND BLACK PEPPER

SERVES 8

1 Melt the butter in a heavy-based saucepan over a medium heat. Add the onions and sauté for 5–10 minutes, until soft. Add the thyme, star anise and garlic. Stir for 2 minutes, ensuring the garlic doesn't burn.

2 Add the carrots and hot stock. Simmer for 20–25 minutes, until the carrots are tender. Remove the thyme sprigs and star anise and purée until smooth. Stir through the cream and season with salt and pepper to taste.

ROAST GARLIC and POTATO SOUP

2 GARLIC BULBS

OLIVE OIL

SALT AND FRESHLY GROUND BLACK PEPPER

3 SPRIGS OF THYME

50G BUTTER

150G ONIONS, ROUGHLY CHOPPED

900G POTATOES, PEELED AND CUBED

850ML STOCK OR WATER

100ML CREAM OR MILK

CRÈME FRAÎCHE, TO GARNISH

SERVES 6–8

1 Preheat the oven to 200°C.

2 Slice the tops off the garlic bulbs. Place the bulbs on a sheet of tinfoil, drizzle with olive oil and season with salt and pepper. Tuck the thyme sprigs in amongst the garlic and gather up the edges of the tinfoil to make a sealed parcel. Cook for 40–50 minutes, until the garlic is soft and sweet. Once it's cool, squeeze the bulbs to remove the purée – simply mashing the bulbs with a fork removes most of the purée easily.

3 Melt the butter in a heavy-based saucepan over a medium heat. Add the onions and sauté for 5–10 minutes, until soft. Add the potatoes and stir to coat in the melted butter. Pour over the stock and add the garlic purée. Bring to the boil and simmer for 10–15 minutes, until the potatoes are cooked. Blitz until smooth, then pour in the cream and season to taste. Garnish with a dollop of crème fraîche.

CLASSIC EGG MAYONNAISE

6 LARGE EGGS

1½ TBSP MAYONNAISE

½ TSP DIJON MUSTARD

SALT AND FRESHLY GROUND
BLACK PEPPER

MAKES 12

1 Place the eggs in a saucepan and add enough cold water to cover the eggs by 3cm. Bring to the boil, remove from the heat, cover the pan and leave to stand for 12 minutes. Remove the eggs from the water and run under cold water to cool them quickly.

2 Once cooled, peel the eggs and cut in half lengthways. Remove the yolks and mash them with the mayonnaise, mustard, salt and pepper. Spoon the yolk mixture back into the whites and serve immediately.

BEETROOT and FENNEL EGGS

1 Place the eggs in a saucepan and add enough cold water to cover the eggs by 3cm. Bring to the boil, remove from the heat, cover the pan and leave to stand for 12 minutes. Remove the eggs from the water and run under cold water to cool them quickly. Once cooled, peel the eggs.

2 Blitz the beetroot and 50ml water with 1½ teaspoons of the fennel seeds and a pinch of salt. Pour into a deep bowl.

3 Immerse the peeled eggs into the beetroot purée. Cover with cling film and place in the fridge for at least 30 minutes, or longer if possible. Remove the eggs from the beetroot purée and rinse under cold water to remove any excess beetroot. The whites will have turned a dramatic pink.

4 Cut each egg in half lengthways. Remove the yolks and mash them with the mayonnaise, the remaining ½ teaspoon fennel seeds and some salt and pepper. Spoon the yolk mixture back into the whites and serve immediately.

6 LARGE EGGS

500G PRE-COOKED BEETROOT

2 TSP FENNEL SEEDS, TOASTED AND FINELY CRUSHED

SALT AND FRESHLY GROUND BLACK PEPPER

1½ TBSP MAYONNAISE

MAKES 12

SPICED CORIANDER EGGS

6 LARGE EGGS

2 TBSP MAYONNAISE

1 TBSP VERY FINELY CHOPPED
FRESH CORIANDER

1/2 TSP CUMIN SEEDS, TOASTED
AND GROUND

1/4 TSP CHILLI POWDER

MAKES 12

1 Place the eggs in a saucepan and add enough cold water to cover the eggs by 3cm. Bring to the boil, remove from the heat, cover the pan and leave to stand for 12 minutes. Remove the eggs from the water and run under cold water to cool them quickly.

2 Once cooled, peel the eggs and cut in half lengthways. Remove the yolks and mash them with the mayonnaise, coriander and spices until smooth. Spoon the yolk mixture back into the whites and serve immediately.

WASABI and TOASTED SESAME SEED EGGS

1 Place the eggs in a saucepan and add enough cold water to cover the eggs by 3cm. Bring to the boil, remove from the heat, cover the pan and leave to stand for 12 minutes. Remove the eggs from the water and run under cold water to cool them quickly.

2 Once cooled, peel the eggs and cut in half lengthways. Remove the yolks and mash them with the mayonnaise, wasabi and salt to taste. Spoon the yolk mixture back into the whites, sprinkle with sesame seeds and serve immediately.

6 LARGE EGGS

2 TBSP MAYONNAISE

½–1 TSP WASABI POWDER, DEPENDING ON ITS STRENGTH

SALT

1 TBSP SESAME SEEDS, TOASTED

MAKES 12

CRAB and CHIVE EGGS

6 LARGE EGGS

2 TBSP MAYONNAISE

2 TBSP WHITE CRABMEAT

1 TBSP FINELY CHOPPED CHIVES,
PLUS EXTRA TO GARNISH

SALT AND FRESHLY GROUND
BLACK PEPPER

1 Place the eggs in a saucepan and add enough cold water to cover the eggs by 3cm. Bring to the boil, remove from the heat, cover the pan and leave to stand for 12 minutes. Remove the eggs from the water and run under cold water to cool them quickly.

2 Once cooled, peel the eggs and cut in half lengthways. Remove the yolks and mash them with the mayonnaise, crabmeat, chives and salt and pepper to taste. Spoon the yolk mixture back into the whites, sprinkle with some snipped chives and serve immediately.

TEA BREAK and DESSERTS

LOOK OUTSIDE! IT'S BEGINNING TO RAIN, SO YOU MIGHT AS WELL STAY FOR DESSERT.

Oh, give in to the longing for something nice ... a treat! You're at the right place because there's creamy, fruity and chocolatey here, a glorious trinity. Let's be honest: you need a wedge of cake to go with that pot of tea. And we have just the one – take a look at that **COFFEE STREUSEL CAKE**! Or how about the thick and creamy **NEW YORK STYLE CHEESECAKE** with a few blueberries and cream? We have plenty of mini cakes too. These precious little single servings are perfect for the lone diner sipping hot coffee with their head stuck in a book. A **BLUEBERRY AND LIME TEACAKE** or a **HONEY AND BROWN BUTTER FINANCIER** just completes the picture. Children go crazy for our range of miniature Victoria sponges, like the **ST CLEMENT'S CAKES**. These little citrus sandwiches are as cute as they are tasty. Perfect for afternoon tea.

For dessert, why not try a bowl of luxurious **CHOCOLATE SOUP**, served with crunchy hazelnut biscotti, toasted brioche or orange cake? There's a creamy **FRUIT FOOL** here to suit everyone, making the most of seasonal rhubarb and blackcurrant. My desert island dessert would have to be the **ORANGE AND PASSIONFRUIT CREAM POTS**. Easy to make and even easier to eat, these beauties' creamy interior is hidden with a speckled passionfruit topping. Are you a busy and important person who loves ice cream and coffee, but doesn't have time for both? The **AFFOGATO** was made for you – a scoop of rich vanilla ice cream drenched in freshly brewed espresso. Or inject a little drama into the evening's proceedings: order the **SICILIAN WEDDING CAKE** and we'll assemble it at your table!

Whether it's tea break or dessert, it's time to surrender to the stunningly sweet dreams ahead.

HONEY and BROWN BUTTER FINANCIERS

Begin this recipe the night before.

80G BUTTER

110G ICING SUGAR

40G PLAIN FLOUR

40G GROUND ALMONDS

¼ TSP BAKING POWDER

4 LARGE EGG WHITES

2 TSP HONEY, PLUS EXTRA TO SERVE

SOFTLY WHIPPED CREAM, TO SERVE

MAKES 24

1 Begin these cakes the night before. First, prepare the beurre noisette. Heat the butter in a saucepan. As it boils, the milk solids will drop to the bottom of the pan and turn golden brown. Remove from the heat once the butter is golden brown and strain through a metal sieve lined with muslin.

2 Mix all the dry ingredients together in a large bowl. In a separate bowl, whisk the hot strained butter with 2 egg whites and the honey, then whisk in the remaining 2 egg whites. Make a well in the centre of the dry ingredients and gently fold in the wet ingredients until uniformly mixed. Cover the batter and refrigerate overnight.

3 The next day, preheat the oven to 180°C. Grease and flour a 24-cup mini-muffin tin.

4 Spoon the batter into the cups, filling each half full. Bake for 10–11 minutes, or until the financiers are lightly golden brown. Cool in the tin for 10 minutes, then transfer to a rack. Top with a little whipped cream and a drizzle of honey.

COFFEE STREUSEL CAKE

FOR THE CAKE:

225G CASTER SUGAR

110G BUTTER, SOFTENED

2 EGGS

300G PLAIN FLOUR

1 TSP BAKING SODA

1 TSP BAKING POWDER

300ML GREEK YOGHURT

75ML STRONG COFFEE, COOLED

FOR THE STREUSEL:

60G CHOPPED WALNUTS, ALMONDS AND BRAZIL NUTS

30G CASTER SUGAR

30G DEMERARA SUGAR OR LIGHT BROWN SUGAR

FOR THE ICING:

200G ICING SUGAR, SIEVED

2 TSP COFFEE ESSENCE (OR 2 TSP INSTANT COFFEE DISSOLVED IN 2 TBSP BOILING WATER)

50G WALNUTS, BRAZIL NUTS OR ALMONDS, TOASTED AND CHOPPED

SERVES 8–10

1 Preheat the oven to 180°C. Grease and flour a 25cm Bundt tin.

2 Combine all the streusel ingredients in a small bowl and set aside.

3 To make the cake, beat together the sugar and butter in a mixer until it's light and creamy. Add the eggs one at a time, beating well after each addition.

4 In a separate bowl, stir together the flour, baking soda and baking powder. Add to the creamed mixture, alternating with the yoghurt and coffee. Mix until just combined.

5 Spoon half the batter into the greased and floured tin and sprinkle with the streusel. Dollop the rest of the batter on top and smooth with the back of a spoon. Bake for 40–45 minutes, until a toothpick inserted in the middle of the cake comes out clean. Leave to cool for 15 minutes in the tin before turning out onto a rack to cool completely.

6 To make the icing, stir the icing sugar and coffee together until it's as thick as honey. Spoon over the top of the cake, letting it drizzle down over the sides. Top with the chopped toasted nuts.

RASPBERRY and COCONUT BUNS

FOR THE BUNS:

300G PLAIN FLOUR

200G BUTTER, MELTED

150G CASTER SUGAR

75G DESICCATED COCONUT

300ML COCONUT MILK

2 TBSP MILK

1 TSP BAKING POWDER

1 TSP VANILLA

2 TBSP RASPBERRY JAM

FOR THE ICING:

300G ICING SUGAR

50ML COCONUT MILK

3 TBSP DESICCATED COCONUT, TOASTED

6–12 RASPBERRIES

MAKES 6 EXTRA-LARGE BUNS OR
12 REGULAR BUNS

1 Preheat the oven to 180°C. Grease and flour the muffin tin wells.

2 Mix together the flour, melted butter, sugar, coconut, coconut milk, milk, baking powder and vanilla in a large bowl.

3 Divide half the batter between the wells. Place 1 teaspoon of jam into each one and spoon over the remaining batter.

4 Bake large buns for 18–20 minutes or regular-sized buns for 25–30 minutes, or until set and golden. Turn out onto a rack to cool completely.

5 To make the icing, sieve the icing sugar into a medium bowl. Gradually add the coconut milk, whisking until the icing is as thick as honey. You may not need all of the milk. Pour the icing over the cooled cakes, sprinkle with toasted coconut and top with a raspberry.

BLUEBERRY and LIME TEACAKES

1 Preheat the oven to 180°C. Grease and flour a 12-cup muffin tin.

2 Beat the butter, sugar and lime zest in a mixer until light and creamy. Add the eggs one at a time, beating well after each addition. Gently mix in the flour along with the milk and lime juice. Fold half the blueberries into the batter, then spoon the batter into the prepared muffin tin. Sink a few blueberries into each well.

3 Bake for 15–20 minutes, until golden and a skewer inserted into the middle comes out clean. Transfer to a rack to cool.

175G BUTTER, SOFTENED

175G CASTER SUGAR

ZEST AND JUICE OF 1 LIME

2 LARGE EGGS

200G SELF-RAISING FLOUR, SIEVED

2 TBSP MILK

200G BLUEBERRIES

MAKES 12

ST CLEMENT'S CAKES

1 Preheat the oven to 180°C. Grease and flour two 12-hole shallow bun tins.

2 Beat the sugar, butter and lemon and orange zests in a mixer until pale and creamy. Add in the eggs one at a time, beating well after each addition. Gently mix in the flour.

3 Divide the batter between the 2 tins. Use a teaspoon to smooth the centre of the cakes so they won't rise too much. Bake for 12–15 minutes, or until a skewer comes out clean when inserted into the centre of each cake. Leave in the tin for a minute before transferring to a cooling rack.

4 To make the icing, beat the icing sugar, butter and zest in a mixer. Loosen the mix with a little lemon or orange juice and whip until it's light and fluffy. Transfer the icing to a piping bag fitted with a star-shaped nozzle. Pipe the icing onto the base of 12 cakes. Sandwich the remaining cakes on top and dust with icing sugar.

FOR THE CAKES:

175G CASTER SUGAR

175G BUTTER, SOFTENED

ZEST OF 1 LEMON

ZEST OF 1 ORANGE

3 LARGE EGGS

175G SELF-RAISING FLOUR, SIEVED

FOR THE ICING:

400G ICING SUGAR, SIEVED, PLUS EXTRA TO DECORATE

200G BUTTER, SOFTENED

FINELY GRATED ZEST AND JUICE OF 1 LEMON OR 1 ORANGE

MAKES 12

OPTIONS:

BLACKCURRANT COULIS:

Place 300g blackcurrants in a bowl, cover with 100g caster sugar and leave to macerate for 30 minutes. Blitz with a hand-held blender until smooth. Sieve into a bowl, pressing the mixture with the back of a spoon to extract maximum juice. Pour over the cooled cheesecake just before serving.

NEW YORK STYLE CHEESECAKE

1 Preheat the oven to 180°C. Lightly grease a 23cm springform tin with butter.

2 Sprinkle the biscuit crumbs over the base of the tin.

3 Beat the cream cheese and sugar in a mixing bowl until well combined. Add the eggs one by one, ensuring it's evenly mixed after each addition. Lastly, add the vanilla extract and stir until smooth.

4 Gently pour the mixture over the biscuit crumbs. Place the springform tin in a large roasting tin and fill the roasting tin with hot water until it comes halfway up the side of the springform tin. Carefully place in the oven and bake for 40–50 minutes, until the top is slightly golden and a skewer inserted into the centre comes out clean. Place on a wire rack to cool.

5 Once the cake is cool enough, remove it from the tin, using a round-bladed knife around the edges if necessary. Place on a serving plate, dust with icing sugar and serve with cold whipped cream and fresh berries.

100G DIGESTIVE BISCUITS, BROKEN INTO CRUMBS

900G CREAM CHEESE

225G CASTER SUGAR

----

4 EGGS

----

1 TSP PURE VANILLA EXTRACT OR VANILLA PASTE

ICING SUGAR, TO SERVE

WHIPPED CREAM, TO SERVE

FRESH BERRIES, TO SERVE

SERVES 10–12

MANGO and LIME FOOL

3 RIPE MANGOS, PEELED AND DICED

ZEST AND JUICE OF 3 LIMES

400ML CREAM

150ML GREEK YOGHURT

2 TBSP LIGHT BROWN SUGAR

3 TBSP DESICCATED COCONUT;
TOASTED

COCONUT BISCUITS (PAGE 147),
TO SERVE

SERVES 6

1 Blitz the diced mangoes and lime juice in a food processor until smooth.

2 In a separate bowl, whip the cream until it's thick and voluminous. Fold in the yoghurt and brown sugar. Stir through half the mango purée.

3 Line up 6 glasses and spoon some purée into the bottom of each glass. Top with the whipped cream and continue to layer and swirl the two together. Cover and place in the fridge to set further.

4 Before serving, top with the toasted coconut and lime zest. Serve with Coconut Biscuits (page 147).

ELDERFLOWER and GOOSEBERRY FOOL

1 Place the gooseberries in a saucepan and pour over the cordial. Simmer the berries in the cordial for 4–5 minutes, until they burst. Allow to cool.

2 In a separate bowl, whip the cream until it's thick and voluminous, then fold in the yoghurt. Stir through half the poached gooseberries and a little of the cordial they were poached in.

3 Line up 6 glasses and spoon some berries into the bottom of each glass. Top with the cream and continue to layer and swirl the cream and berries together. Cover and place in the fridge until ready to serve.

4 Top with a light scattering of elderflower petals.

1KG GOOSEBERRIES

250ML ELDERFLOWER CORDIAL

400ML CREAM

150ML GREEK YOGHURT

ELDERFLOWER PETALS, TO DECORATE

SERVES 6

RHUBARB, ROSE and PISTACHIO FOOL

FOR THE FOOL:

650G RHUBARB, ROUGHLY CHOPPED

100G GOLDEN CASTER SUGAR

400ML CREAM

150ML GREEK YOGHURT

1/2 TSP ROSEWATER

FOR THE CANDIED PISTACHIOS:

1 1/2 TSP GRANULATED SUGAR

60G SHELLED PISTACHIOS

1 TBSP DEMERARA SUGAR

SERVES 6

1 First, make the candied pistachios. Preheat the oven to 180°C. Line a baking tray with greaseproof paper.

2 Stir the granulated sugar with 1½ tsp hot water in a bowl until the sugar dissolves. Add the pistachios and Demerara sugar and stir to coat the nuts with the sugar. Spread the pistachios on the tray and bake for about 8 minutes, until crisp. Allow to cool, then break into pieces.

3 Place the rhubarb in a pan with the golden caster sugar. Cover and heat gently for about 5 minutes, until the rhubarb is just tender. Remove the lid and increase the heat so the juice thickens. Taste and add more sugar if necessary. Leave to cool, then drain the rhubarb and reserve the juice.

4 Whip the cream until it's thick and voluminous. Fold in the yoghurt and rosewater, then gently fold in the drained rhubarb. Divide between 6 glasses. Cover and place in the fridge until ready to serve.

5 Pour the reserved juice over the top of each glass and scatter over some candied pistachios.

BLACKCURRANT and MINT FOOL

1 Cover the blackcurrants and mint with the sugar and leave to macerate for 30 minutes. Remove the mint leaves and blitz the blackcurrants with a hand-held blender until smooth. Sieve into a bowl, pressing the mixture with the back of a spoon to extract maximum juice.

2 In a separate bowl, whip the cream until it's thick and voluminous. Fold in the yoghurt. Gently ripple half the blackcurrant coulis through the cream mixture. Spoon into 6 glasses and layer with the remaining coulis. Cover and place in the fridge until ready to serve.

3 Top with additional blackcurrants and a sprig of mint.

300G BLACKCURRANTS, PLUS EXTRA TO DECORATE

4 LARGE MINT LEAVES, PLUS EXTRA TO DECORATE

100G CASTER SUGAR

400ML CREAM

150ML GREEK YOGHURT

SERVES 6

Just to balance my absolute adoration of all things dairy, I've included my vegan chocolate mousse recipe. There are plenty of different versions of this around, but I find it's nicest when kept simple: a perfectly ripe avocado, blitzed until creamy with cacao and sweetened with agave syrup. It was the perfect dessert for me when I was pregnant, as it contained no raw egg, as most mousses do. It was also rich in antioxidants from the cacao and provided valuable fats from the avocado. It would have been irresponsible of me not to have eaten this on a regular basis!

4 PERFECTLY RIPE AVOCADOS, PITTED

180G 100% CACAO POWDER OR UNSWEETENED COCOA POWDER

3–4 TBSP AGAVE NECTAR OR HONEY

1 TSP VANILLA EXTRACT

PINCH OF SEA SALT

4 TBSP HAZELNUTS, TOASTED AND CHOPPED

SERVES 4–6

1 Use a stick blender or a food processor to blitz the avocado until smooth. Add the cacao, agave nectar, vanilla extract and a pinch of salt and blend again until thick and smooth.

2 Spoon into individual glasses and chill for at least 1 hour. Sprinkle generously with toasted hazelnuts before serving.

OPTIONS:

Add any one of the following: a pinch of chilli flakes, 1 teaspoon cinnamon, a handful of fresh raspberries, 1 teaspoon peppermint extract, or serve with fresh fruit and berries. If you're not avoiding dairy, then a dollop of softly whipped cream or Greek yoghurt really adds to this dish.

VEGAN CHOCOLATE MOUSSE

ORANGE and PASSIONFRUIT CREAM POTS

4 LARGE EGGS

2 LARGE EGG YOLKS

185G CASTER SUGAR

500ML MILK

250ML CREAM

2 TBSP COINTREAU

1 TSP VANILLA EXTRACT

ZEST OF 1 ORANGE

3 PASSIONFRUIT

SERVES 6–8

1 Preheat the oven to 150°C. Place a tea towel on the base of a high-sided roasting tin to prevent the ramekins from slipping and sliding around in the tin. Arrange 6 x 150ml ramekins on top of the tea towel.

2 Beat the eggs, yolks and sugar until thick and pale. Add the milk, cream, Cointreau and vanilla. Pour the mixture through a fine sieve to make it a little less voluminous. Stir the orange zest into the custard, then carefully pour into the ramekins. Transfer the roasting tin to the oven shelf and carefully pour boiling water in until it reaches halfway up the sides of the ramekins.

3 Bake for 35–40 minutes, or until set. Once cooled, top each ramekin with the seeds from half a passionfruit. Serve chilled or at room temperature. These can be made a day ahead and kept in the fridge.

CHOCOLATE SOUP

350ML CREAM

350ML MILK

180G MILK CHOCOLATE,
ROUGHLY CHOPPED

100G DARK CHOCOLATE,
ROUGHLY CHOPPED

SERVES 6

Pour the cream and milk into a heavy-based pan and bring to a simmer over a low heat. Add the roughly chopped chocolate and whisk constantly for about 4 minutes, or until all the chocolate has melted and the soup is thick and smooth. Remove from the heat and add a liqueur of your choice. Keep warm or serve immediately.

OPTIONS:
○ Add 2 tbsp Cointreau and serve with orange cake.
○ Add 2 tbsp Baileys and serve with toasted brioche.
○ Serve with digestive or oat biscuits.

EASY RASPBERRY and LIQUEUR CHEESECAKE POTS

Divide the crushed digestives between 2 glasses. Stir the liqueur through the yoghurt. Place half the raspberries on top of the biscuit base. Spoon over the yoghurt and top with the remaining raspberries. Serve immediately.

OPTIONS:

Use whatever liqueur or biscuits you prefer. Cointreau pairs well with chocolate digestives and Greek yoghurt. An amaretti biscuit base is sweet and crunchy, or use plain oatcakes if you're feeling virtuous.

100G DIGESTIVE BISCUITS OR OATCAKES, CRUSHED

----

2 TBSP BAILEYS OR ANY IRISH CREAM LIQUEUR

200ML VANILLA YOGHURT

200G RASPBERRIES

MAKES 2

Chocolate Soup

Easy Raspberry and Liqueur Cheesecake Pots

GINGER and WHITE CHOCOLATE FLAPJACKS

1 Preheat the oven to 150°C. Lightly grease and line a 20cm x 30cm baking tin.

2 Place the butter, sugar and syrup into a large saucepan and heat gently until the butter has melted, stirring occasionally. Remove the pan from the heat and add the oats, white chocolate and ginger. Stir thoroughly to mix.

3 Pour the mixture into the prepared tin. Use the back of a spoon to level the surface and press down the mixture.

4 Bake for 40–50 minutes in the centre of the oven. Leave to cool in the tin before cutting into 12–15 bars. Store in an airtight tin for up to 1 week.

225G BUTTER

150G LIGHT BROWN SUGAR

2 TBSP SYRUP FROM PRESERVED GINGER (OR HONEY, MAPLE SYRUP OR GOLDEN SYRUP)

350G PORRIDGE OATS

100G WHITE CHOCOLATE, CHOPPED INTO CHUNKS

4 NUGGETS OF PRESERVED GINGER, FINELY CHOPPED

MAKES 12–15 BARS

AFFOGATO

Possibly one of the nicest ways to end a meal and also the most delicious! Affogato, which means 'drowned' in Italian, consists of vanilla ice cream in a pool of hot coffee. The contrasting hot and cold and the sweet, creamy ice cream with the strong, bitter coffee is hard to beat.

1 For 6 people, you'll need 1 litre of good-quality vanilla ice cream. Place 1 generous scoop of ice cream into each serving glass or cup. Pour a long shot of freshly brewed espresso coffee over each scoop and serve immediately.

2 For a special occasion, a shot of Frangelico, the hazelnut-flavoured liqueur, adds to this immensely. Baileys or Tia Maria can also be used. I like the traditional vanilla ice cream best for this, but a good-quality chocolate ice cream can be used to create a mocha affogato.

COCONUT BISCUITS

1 Preheat the oven to 180°C. Line 2 large baking trays with greaseproof paper.

2 Put everything in a large bowl and stir slowly with a wooden spoon until just combined.

3 Place scant teaspoons of the mixture onto the tray, spacing well apart, as they will spread.

4 Bake for 10–12 minutes, until golden around the edges. Leave on the trays for 5 minutes before placing them on a wire rack to cool.

200G CASTER SUGAR

150G SELF-RAISING FLOUR

110G BUTTER, MELTED

80G DESICCATED COCONUT

1 EGG, LIGHTLY BEATEN

MAKES 25–30 BISCUITS

Sicilian Wedding Cake

SICILIAN WEDDING CAKE

This cake is inspired by one I ate at a wedding a few years ago in Italy.

After an amazingly elaborate meal, a round table covered in a white cloth was brought out and placed centre stage amongst the guests. The chef brought out a huge platter with a biscuit base, several bowls of berries and a large bowl of what looked like clotted cream. The room soon became silent – we were all transfixed by him as he assembled this incredibly theatrical cake. He spread out the creamy mixture, then layers of berries, scattering them generously by hand. Finally, he dotted a few sprigs of mint around the cake and dusted the entire thing with icing sugar. It was the first dessert I had ever seen someone get a standing ovation for!

And not only was it beautiful to look at, the cake tasted amazing too. I just had to figure out what the creamy mixture was. After much research, I discovered a Sicilian cassata cake recipe. Its ricotta-based filling is the closest I've come to recapturing that magical dish.

I made this for guests at one of our supper clubs a few years ago and it had the same dramatic effect as I assembled it in front of everyone!

1 Crush the digestives in a food processor until there are crumbs and some large bits. You don't want dust! Melt the butter and mix well in a large bowl with the biscuit crumbs.

2 Tip the buttered crumbs onto your serving plate. Work quickly while the mixture is still warm. Shape into a large circle or rectangle and make sure it's compact by flattening it with the back of a spoon so that it will set into a nice crunchy biscuit layer that you can cut into.

3 While the base is setting, place the berries in nice serving bowls. Slice the strawberries and sprinkle them with caster sugar.

4 Place the ricotta, lemon zest, icing sugar and vanilla into a bowl and beat until combined.

5 Whip the cream until it's soft. Gently fold the cream into the ricotta mixture using a large spatula.

6 To serve, spread the ricotta cream mixture over the base, top with the berries and dust with icing sugar.

1.5KG DIGESTIVE BISCUITS

750G BUTTER

900G BLACKBERRIES

900G BLUEBERRIES

900G STRAWBERRIES

900G RASPBERRIES

900G REDCURRANTS

1.2KG RICOTTA (6 TUBS)

ZEST OF 4 LEMONS

6 TBSP ICING SUGAR, PLUS EXTRA TO DECORATE

4 TBSP VANILLA ESSENCE

2 LITRES CREAM

SERVES 35–40

SIDES and EXTRAS

THE DREAM DELI LARDER HAS SHELVES THAT REACH THE CEILING.

Next to the many tins of tea leaves and bottles of cordial are jars of magical **DUKKAH**, lined up and ready to be sprinkled on salads, tagines or roast aubergine. Looking for something to take away? Then grab a little jar of our flavoured butters to transform your morning toast or scone. A spoonful of the **WHIPPED HONEY BUTTER** melted onto a freshly made pancake takes the sublime to the ridiculously delicious. If you're more savoury, like myself, then a jar of our homemade **LABNEH** drenched in grassy olive oil will complete your charcuterie board with sophisticated glee.

It's always nice to change it up with a little extra something on the side. These are the little touches that will make a meal, like **MINT AND PEA PURÉE** with grilled fish or **BUTTERBEAN MASH** with a flame-grilled rib-eye steak. How about a trio of salads and a dollop of **TZATZIKI** with your lamb chop? If you're stuck in limbo between lunch and dinner, then order one of the many types of **HUMMUS** with some crunchy vegetable sticks for dipping.

As the day comes to a close in the Dream Deli, we close the shutters, light some candles and dust off the projector. Stay a little longer, as it's time to watch a film! We pass around big bowls of **BAKED KALE CHIPS** and **ROOT VEGETABLE CRISPS**, not to mention our famous **FLAVOURED POPCORNS**: the **SEA SALT, HONEY AND MACADAMIA NUT POPCORN** has become the stuff of legend!

You'll never feel like you've ordered the wrong thing in the Dream Deli – your hands and eyes and cute little tummy will be too busy falling in love!

CAULIFLOWER PURÉE
with BALSAMIC SYRUP

1 LARGE CAULIFLOWER,
DIVIDED INTO FLORETS

50G GRATED PARMESAN

----

2 TBSP CREAM CHEESE OR THICK
GREEK YOGHURT

SALT AND FRESHLY GROUND
BLACK PEPPER

FOR THE BALSAMIC SYRUP:

----

3 TBSP BALSAMIC VINEGAR

----

1 TSP HONEY

SERVES 4

1 First make the balsamic syrup by heating the vinegar and honey in a little pan until it's thick and syrupy. Set aside.

2 Steam the cauliflower or boil in water until it's cooked through. Drain well and try to remove as much water as possible. Purée the cooked cauliflower with the Parmesan and cream cheese. Taste for seasoning. Spoon into a serving bowl and drizzle with the balsamic syrup.

BUTTERBEAN MASH

1 X 400G TIN OF BUTTERBEANS

----

1 CLOVE GARLIC

----

1 SPRIG OF THYME

100ML STOCK OR WATER

----

1 TBSP OLIVE OIL

SALT AND FRESHLY GROUND BLACK PEPPER

SERVES 2

Drain and rinse the butterbeans. Place in a pan with the garlic and thyme. Pour over the stock and place over a medium heat until bubbling and warmed through. Remove the thyme, add the olive oil and blitz until smooth with a hand-held blender. Taste for seasoning.

MINT and PEA PURÉE

400G FROZEN PEAS

10G MINT LEAVES (RESERVE 3 LEAVES)

20G BUTTER

SALT AND FRESHLY GROUND BLACK PEPPER

SERVES 4

Cook the peas in boiling water along with the mint leaves for 3–4 minutes, until the peas are just done. Drain and remove the mint leaves. Return the peas to the pot, then add the butter, season with a little salt and pepper and add 3 fresh mint leaves. Blitz until smooth.

OPTIONS:
This pea purée also works really well with coriander leaves and a little finely chopped red chilli.

BEETROOT and POTATO MASH

Cook the potatoes in boiling water until they're almost done and add the beetroot for the last 5 minutes. Drain well and return to the pan. Add the butter and mash well, until smooth. Add the crème fraîche and mash again, until creamy. Season well with salt and pepper.

OPTIONS:
Add 1 teaspoon fresh horseradish when serving this mash with roast beef or mackerel.

600G POTATOES, PEELED AND CUT INTO LARGE CHUNKS

150G COOKED BEETROOT, CUT INTO LARGE CHUNKS

20G BUTTER

1 TBSP CRÈME FRAÎCHE

SALT AND FRESHLY GROUND BLACK PEPPER

SERVES 4

SEA SALT and PEPPER PATATAS BRAVAS

1 Preheat the oven to 200°C. Place a roasting tray in the oven to warm.

2 Peel the potatoes and cut into 2cm cubes. Place the potato cubes in a sieve and rinse under running water to remove excess starch. Dry with a tea towel.

3 Place the potatoes in a large bowl and pour over the olive oil, mixing well so that each cube is coated.

4 Tip the potatoes into the hot roasting tray and cook for 40–45 minutes, until crisp. Remove any excess oil using kitchen paper, then season with salt and pepper.

250G POTATOES (ROOSTERS WORK WELL)

2–3 TBSP OLIVE OIL

SEA SALT AND FRESHLY-GROUND BLACK PEPPER

SERVES 2

HUMMUS

1 Place the chickpeas, tahini, garlic and lemon juice in a food processor or blitz with a stick blender. Add 100ml cold water and a generous pinch of salt. Blitz until smooth and creamy.

2 Spoon into a serving dish, drizzle with the oil and sprinkle with a pinch of paprika.

OPTIONS:
Smooth peanut butter makes a fine alternative to tahini.

450G COOKED CHICKPEAS

150G TAHINI

2 CLOVES GARLIC

JUICE OF 1 LEMON

PINCH OF SALT

1 TBSP OLIVE OIL

¼ TSP PAPRIKA

SERVES 6

BEETROOT HUMMUS

1 X 400G TIN OF CHICKPEAS, DRAINED (RESERVE
THE WATER FROM THE TIN)
----

1 X 250G PACK PRE-COOKED BEETROOT, DRAINED
AND ROUGHLY CHOPPED

15G CORIANDER, FINELY CHOPPED
----

1 CLOVE GARLIC

SERVES 6

JUICE OF 1 LEMON
----

2 TBSP WATER FROM THE TINNED CHICKPEAS
----

1 TBSP OLIVE OIL
----

1 TBSP TAHINI

SALT, TO TASTE

Place everything in a food processor and blitz until smooth.
Taste and adjust the seasoning.

ROASTED RED PEPPER HUMMUS

2 RED PEPPERS, ROASTED AND DESEEDED

1 X 400G TIN OF CHICKPEAS, DRAINED (RESERVE THE WATER FROM THE TIN)

15G BASIL LEAVES, FINELY CHOPPED

1 CLOVE GARLIC

JUICE OF 1 LEMON

SERVES 6

2 TBSP WATER FROM THE TINNED CHICKPEAS

1 TBSP OLIVE OIL

1 TBSP TAHINI

1 TSP SMOKED PAPRIKA

SALT AND FRESHLY GROUND BLACK PEPPER

Place everything in a food processor and blitz until smooth.
Taste and adjust the seasoning.

DUKKAH

Dukkah is a versatile addition to your store cupboard. It's delicious sprinkled over salads or used as a dip for crusty sourdough along with a grassy olive oil. Try rolling balls of labneh (see page 182) or goat cheese in this flavoursome mix for fantastic results.

100G HAZELNUTS

150G SESAME SEEDS

50G SUNFLOWER SEEDS

1 HEAPED TSP CORIANDER SEEDS

1 HEAPED TSP FENNEL SEEDS

1 HEAPED TSP CUMIN SEEDS

1 TSP BLACK PEPPERCORNS

1 TBSP SMOKED SEA SALT

MAKES 1 JAR

1 Preheat the oven to 180°C.

2 Place the hazelnuts on a baking tray and toast in the hot oven until they're golden and the skin can easily brush off. Once cooled, tip the nuts onto a tea towel and rub until most of the skins have been removed.

3 Toast the sesame seeds in a frying pan over a medium heat until they turn golden. Transfer to a bowl. The sunflower seeds can also be toasted this way and transferred to the bowl.

4 Toast the coriander and fennel seeds in the pan. After about 30 seconds, add the cumin seeds. Remove the seeds from the heat after another few seconds, once they begin to pop.

5 Place the peppercorns in a food processor and blitz briefly before adding the coriander, fennel and cumin seeds and blitzing again. Once the spices are roughly ground, add them to the sesame and sunflower seeds along with the salt. Stir to combine and keep in an airtight container for up to 3 months.

BAKED KALE CHIPS

200G KALE

1 TBSP OLIVE OIL

SEA SALT, TO TASTE

1 Preheat the oven to 150°C.

2 Rinse and dry the kale, then remove the tough stems. Cut the leaves into large pieces, toss with olive oil in a bowl and sprinkle with salt. Arrange in 1 layer on a large baking tray. Bake for 20 minutes, until crisp. Transfer to a wire rack to cool.

ROOT VEGETABLE CRISPS

1 Wash and peel the vegetables. Slice as thinly as possible using a sharp knife or a mandoline. Dry the vegetable slices using kitchen paper. The drier they are, the better they'll fry.

2 Pour the sunflower oil into a large, high-sided pot until it's about 10cm deep. Heat the oil until it reaches about 180°C. You can test it by dropping a vegetable slice in and checking if it sizzles. Working in batches, add in a single layer of vegetable slices and fry for about 3 minutes, or until they turn slightly darker in colour. Remove from the oil and drain on kitchen paper. Sprinkle with salt to taste.

6–7 ROOT VEGETABLES (CARROT, TURNIP, CELERIAC, BEETROOT, PARSNIP, POTATO, SWEET POTATO)

SUNFLOWER OIL

SALT, TO TASTE

BASIC POPCORN

50ML SUNFLOWER OIL

120G POPCORN KERNELS

SALT, TO TASTE

SERVES 6

Heat the oil in a large pot and add a couple of corn kernels. Once they pop, the oil is hot enough. Add the remaining corn kernels and stir to coat. Place a lid on the pot and leave the corn to pop. Once the popping slows, remove the pot from the heat and leave any remaining kernels to pop. Transfer to a bowl and sprinkle with salt.

SEA SALT, HONEY and MACADAMIA NUT POPCORN

1 Heat the brown sugar, butter and honey on a high heat until it's bubbling. Lower the heat and simmer for 1 minute, until syrupy.

2 Place the roughly chopped nuts and the freshly popped corn into a large bowl. Pour the syrup over. Stir well and tip onto a tray lined with greaseproof paper to cool. Sprinkle with sea salt.

90G LIGHT BROWN SUGAR

60G BUTTER

3 TBSP HONEY

110G MACADAMIA NUTS, ROUGHLY CHOPPED

1 BATCH OF BASIC POPCORN (SEE PAGE 174)

SEA SALT FLAKES, SUCH AS IRISH ATLANTIC SEA SALT OR MALDON

SERVES 6

INDIAN SPICED POPCORN

150G FLAKED ALMONDS, TOASTED

50G SULTANAS

50G BUTTER, MELTED

25G DESICCATED COCONUT

1 TBSP GARAM MASALA

1 TSP NIGELLA SEEDS

1 BATCH OF BASIC POPCORN

(SEE PAGE 174)

SERVES 6

Place the almonds, sultanas, melted butter, coconut, garam masala and nigella seeds into a large bowl and stir. Add the freshly popped corn and stir to coat evenly. Serve immediately.

LEMON and THYME POPCORN

Place the melted butter, thyme, Parmesan, lemon zest and some black pepper into a large bowl and stir. Add the freshly popped corn and stir to coat evenly. Serve immediately.

50G BUTTER, MELTED

1 TBSP FINELY CHOPPED THYME

1 TBSP GRATED PARMESAN

½ TBSP LEMON ZEST

FRESHLY GROUND BLACK PEPPER

1 BATCH OF BASIC POPCORN
(SEE PAGE 174)

SERVES 6

HOT ROSEMARY POPCORN

50G BUTTER, MELTED

----

2 TBSP GRATED PARMESAN

----

1 TBSP FINELY CHOPPED ROSEMARY

½ TSP LIGHT BROWN SUGAR

½ TSP CAYENNE PEPPER

----

1 BATCH OF BASIC POPCORN (SEE PAGE 174)

SERVES 6

Place the butter, Parmesan, rosemary, brown sugar and cayenne pepper into a large bowl and stir. Add the freshly popped corn and stir to coat evenly. Serve immediately.

TZATZIKI

1 CUCUMBER

300ML GREEK YOGHURT

1–2 GARLIC CLOVES, CRUSHED

2 TBSP FINELY CHOPPED DILL

SALT

1 TBSP OLIVE OIL

SMOKED PAPRIKA, TO GARNISH

SERVES 4

1 Peel and halve the cucumber. Remove the seeds by running a teaspoon down the centre. Grate it coarsely and place in a sieve over the sink to drain.

2 Combine the yoghurt, crushed garlic, dill and some salt. Loosen the mixture with a little olive oil. Add the drained cucumber and stir. Serve with a drizzle of oil or sprinkle the top with smoked paprika.

OPTIONS:

○ Use finely shredded mint leaves instead of dill.

○ Add lemon juice or zest to give it a citrus kick.

LABNEH

400ML GREEK YOGHURT

½ TSP SALT

1 TBSP OLIVE OIL

FRESHLY CHOPPED HERBS, TO SERVE

DUKKAH, TO SERVE

SERVES 6

1 Place a piece of muslin or cheesecloth into a large sieve set over a bowl. Stir the salt through the yoghurt, then spoon the yoghurt into the centre of the cloth and gather up the sides. Tie the four corners into a knot and hang over the bowl for 24–48 hours. I usually tie the cloth to the handle of a kitchen cabinet or onto the tap. The liquid will slowly drip down into the bowl, leaving a thick, crumbly yet creamy cheese.

2 Transfer the cheese to a serving bowl and pour a little olive oil over the top. Scatter with freshly chopped herbs or dukkah (see page 168).

3 You can also roll this cheese into little balls, then store them a jar, covered with oil. Or roll the balls in chopped nuts, dukkah, dried chilli flakes, smoked paprika or chopped herbs.

CRISPY FRIED SHALLOTS

1 Heat the oil in a small saucepan until it reaches 150°C or until a cube of bread fries when it's dropped in the oil. Add the shallots and cook for about 8 minutes, until golden brown. Use a slotted spoon to remove the shallots and leave to drain on kitchen paper. Sprinkle with a little salt.

2 These are best used the day they are made. Use in salads or to garnish soups, and they're also delicious with mashed potatoes. Keep the strained shallot-flavoured oil in a bottle in the fridge and use for salad dressings, etc.

225ML RAPESEED OIL

4 LARGE OR 6 SMALL SHALLOTS, THINLY SLICED

SEA SALT

BERRY BUTTER

110G BUTTER, SOFTENED

----

1 TSP LEMON JUICE

----

1 TBSP HONEY OR AGAVE SYRUP

30G BERRIES (RASPBERRIES, STRAWBERRIES OR BLACKBERRIES)

Whip the butter and lemon juice together until light and creamy. Add the honey and mix until combined. Finally, add the berries and mix until they're just softened and roughly mixed for a rippled effect, or mix for longer to get a smooth, even-coloured butter. Spoon into little bowls or wrap in rolls of greaseproof paper and keep in the fridge or freezer. Bring to room temperature before using.

WHIPPED HONEY BUTTER

Whip the butter and honey until soft and creamy. Add the vanilla and mix until just combined. Spoon into a bowl or jar and keep in the fridge. Bring to room temperature before using.

110G BUTTER, SOFTENED

75G HONEY

½ VANILLA BEAN OR ½ TSP VANILLA EXTRACT

OPTIONS:

○ Use maple syrup instead of honey and add some toasted and roughly chopped pecan nuts to this butter to make an incredible topping for pancakes and waffles.

○ Add 1 teaspoon ground cinnamon to the honey butter and use it to fry pancakes or spread on hot toast.

ORANGE BLOSSOM BUTTER

110G BUTTER, SOFTENED

60G HONEY

----

4 TSP ORANGE ZEST

½ TSP ORANGE BLOSSOM WATER

Whip the butter and honey until soft and creamy. Add the orange zest and orange blossom water and mix until just combined. Spoon into a bowl or jar and keep in the fridge. Bring to room temperature before using.

FROZEN HERB CUBES

For me, herbs are an incredibly important part of cooking. Almost every savoury meal I cook contains herbs – they inject a real freshness and pack a flavoursome punch.

It may seem a little melodramatic to be preserving herbs when we can get them fresh no matter what the season in our local supermarket, but I find this method of preservation invaluable when I have lots of leftover dill or when the herb bed has a particularly productive summer. Home-grown herbs suspended in butter bring sunshine to glum winter nights when melted over steaks or fish. I find thyme the best herb to have frozen. Winter warmers like spaghetti Bolognese, lasagne, shepherd's pie or stews all benefit from one of these little thyme cubes. They're also fantastic in soups, sauces or gravy. Dill is also great, as it's not something I would regularly have fresh. A foil-wrapped salmon darne is transformed when baked with a butter and dill cube. I like to add finely chopped rosemary and chilli flake butter cubes to rustic potato wedges as they finish roasting. And the traditional combination of thyme and lemon zest is perfect for roast chicken.

Simply choose good-quality herbs, chop them finely and pack into an ice cube tray until two-thirds full. Then pour olive oil or melted butter over the herbs, cover with cling film and freeze overnight. Once frozen solid, they can be popped out of the ice cube trays and stored in small ziplock bags. Label with the date and herb/oil type.

INDEX

PHOTO CREDITS